All Scripture references taken from the KJV of the Holy Bible, unless otherwise indicated.

INTO FREEDOM: *Reclaiming Your Authority From Spiritual Knots*

by Dr. Marlene Miles

Freshwater Press 2026

Freshwaterpress9@gmail.com

ISBN: 978-1-971933-28-3

Paperback Version

Copyright 2026, Dr. Marlene Miles

All rights reserved. No part of this book may be reproduced, distributed, or transmitted by any means or in any means including photocopying, recording or other electronic or mechanical methods without prior written permission of the publisher except in the case of brief publications or critical reviews.

Table of Contents

Stand fast therefore in the liberty wherewith Christ hath made us free, and be not entangled again with the yoke of bondage.

Galatians 5:1

INTO FREEDOM

Reclaiming Your Spirit From Invisible Knots

PART I — RECOGNITION

(Before You Knew You Were Entangled)

You don't wake up one morning and decide to tie your life in knots.

Entanglement begins quietly. A thread here. A role there. A connection that feels natural. A responsibility that feels noble.

You didn't intend to become bound. You intended to love well.

Recognition is not accusation. It is the moment you notice that something once flexible has tightened.

This section names what you felt before you had language for it.

I'M NOT STUCK, *AM I?*

Tina remembers the days when everything used to work. If she thought of something, she could easily accomplish it. If she wanted to lose 5 pounds by Friday—no problem. When she prayed, she got answers. She now wonders that maybe she took it all for granted and now it's changed. She looked to see what had changed in her life since she first noticed these differences. Seems she works all the time, these days. She doesn't walk as much as she used to. She has a car now and drives everywhere so she finds that she's gaining weight. There's a pound being added here and there, all of a sudden.

Things she wants to do, she doesn't do or can't do anymore. She's in a flat dead end job. Her parents don't even help her out like they used to.

Why?

Tina states that the only difference is Brad. That is the only difference in her life. *Sure, he pays a lot of attention to me. Sure, he wants to see me every day so I don't have that much time for my parents and friends like I used to. Brad calls me every morning, and night, and all day, but that's just because he cares.* He's starting a new business and I give him a little help from time to time; isn't it classy for a woman to take a man out to dinner and pay? That shows she's into him, right? But for some reason, say Tina, "I feel stuck."

Okay, Tina thinks, Now that I see what's going on, I can make some changes and get things back to normal, back on track, *right*?

There is a moment that comes after struggle but before collapse when a person realizes something quieter and more dangerous. *I thought I was moving... but nothing is actually changing.*

This is not rebellion or failure. This is stalled purpose masked as effort. People can remain busy, committed, faithful, disciplined and still be standing in place.

Even though in motion, that is not proof of progress. Motion can be mindless and unproductive. Sometimes people busy themselves with mindless labor. Effort is not evidence of direction, and sincerity does not guarantee movement. You can be showing up, trying hard, staying loyal, repeating patterns, but still just expending energy because inertia is governing the project or the day.

The most dangerous part of being stuck is that **it often feels like movement**. Routine feels like momentum. Endurance feels like advancement. Familiar resistance feels like warfare.

Then one day, you notice like a cartoon reel, the scenery hasn't changed. You may realize that the outcomes repeat. The same conversations recur, and the same limits remain. Then the question surfaces, *Why am I not arriving anywhere? Where are my breakthroughs? When will things change? When will I see success in this matter?*

There's an old joke where Bill Cosby said he went jogging, looked down, and noticed his shadow wasn't running. Sometimes any of us could mistake intention for motion. The body believes it's running, but the evidence says otherwise.

This kind of stoppage is not caused by lack of effort, lack of faith, or lack of sincerity. It is caused by misaligned authority. Real movement requires direction, permission, governance, and release. If authority is deferred, fragmented, abdicated, and overridden. Then motion freezes — even while activity continues. That's why people can be exhausted without ever advancing.

You know you're no longer moving when your effort increases, but your authority does not. At that point more striving won't help, more loyalty won't help, and more endurance won't help. Only realignment will.

In this case, noticing is actually progress. The moment you *notice* you are not moving is the first moment you actually are. Noticing breaks illusion. Illusion is what keeps people stuck longest; this is not despair; this is clarity returning.

You must finally notice when you are no longer moving. There is a moment that comes after struggle but before collapse. when a person realizes something quieter and more dangerous:

I thought I was moving... but nothing is actually changing.

This is not rebellion or failure. This is stalled purpose masked as effort. People can remain busy, committed, faithful, disciplined, and still be standing in place.

Motion is not proof of progress. Effort is not evidence of direction. Sincerity does not guarantee movement. You can be showing up, trying hard, staying loyal, repeating patterns, expending energy, and still be governed by inertia.

Before you know it, it's five years later, or 10 years later, and what have you done? What have you accomplished? Routine feels like momentum. For the Israelites, it was 40 years later.

Endurance feels like advancement. Familiar resistance feels like warfare. Until one day, you notice that the scenery hasn't changed, the outcomes repeat, the same conversations recur, the same limits remain. And that's when the question surfaces — usually quietly, *Why am I not arriving anywhere?*

PART II — DIAGNOSIS

(The Anatomy of the Knot)

Once you sense that something is wrong, the instinct is to fix it. Knots do not respond to effort. They respond to structure.

Before separation, there must be clarity. Before freedom, there must be diagnosis.

This section exposes the threads, the patterns, and the architecture of entanglement — not to shame you, but to show you that what felt mysterious was actually structured.

You are not crazy. You are not weak. You were woven. And what is woven can be unwoven.

THE ANATOMY OF THE KNOT

Most people can point to the moment they felt their peace shift. It was not when someone broke their heart or when a relationship went bad. It was not when they were betrayed. But it was when something subtle slipped into their spirit —a pull, a fog, a weight, a confusion, a distraction, a tightening. It wasn't dramatic, loud or even obvious.

It was a knot.

It may have been a spiritual knot, or an emotional knot. It could have been a mental knot. No matter the type, it was a knot and it was in the unseen realm. Cords and ropes and fibers touching, connecting, intertwining and then looping and tightening; that is what creates the knot.

Entanglements lock in place. An entanglement becomes "set" when The mind assigns a role and then the emotions submit. The spirit gets entangled in the confusion. The atmosphere becomes charged. Communication deepens unnecessarily. Access becomes habitual. At that point, you usually don't WANT the person, no-- you're just caught in the tangle. This may be the time when you ask yourself why do you stay with them but then resign yourself to you don't know why but you can't break up or break it off with them.

That may be the day, the moment that knot began dictating the flow of your emotions, the direction of your thoughts, and the clarity of your discernment.

Not every form of bondage is heavy. Sometimes it's tangled. When it comes to captivity and bondage, there are chains you can feel, there are cages you can see. But knots? Knots hide. They are designed to be disguised and also hidden but lockable. Knots disguise themselves as concern, compassion, loyalty, curiosity, obligation, connection, "just checking in." They are disguised as, "I don't know why they're on my mind" and maybe I am on their mind too. Most likely they are not, but that is a lie that is told online and in many other places. Intrusive, obsessive, "can't let go" thoughts. Some people can't let go of anything, good or bad. Knots are evident in the person who "needs closure" as if they know what closure really is or if they really want it. I think of the person who needs to see that other person "just one more time", you know, "for closure."

If you still want to see them, that's not a desire for closure, it is a desire to see them.

Knots don't show up looking like bondage; they show up looking like something you think you should examine, protect, manage, understand, or resolve.

But here is the truth: A knot is not a relationship. A knot is not a covenant. A knot is a constriction. A knot decreases movement. A knot limits circulation. A knot restricts flow and absorbs energy. A knot interrupts direction; it ties you down.

In the natural world, a rope with a knot in it loses both flexibility and reach.

In the spirit, a person with even one knot in themselves loses clarity, discernment, peace, focus, emotional authenticity, and identity alignment.

You are not stuck, not really; you are tangled, and tangled people always feel spiritually "off," but can't articulate why.

That is one of the reasons I wrote the book, **ENTANGLEMENTS**, so discussions and descriptions about entanglement can be articulated. It is so understanding can be reached and knowledge of modes and systems can be had, since knowledge is power and we need power over evil and everything that tries to take power over us.

Years ago, I wrote a book entitled, *The Threefold Cord. In it I discussed* a revelation of what God *binds*. But as we know there is a weed for every beautiful flower; the devil counterfeits any and everything that God has put in place. God binds, so the evil one has tried to copy that to the negative.

God binds through covenant, with clarity and in purpose. God divinely joins. There is agreement and alignment with synergy, shared assignment and no hidden agendas.

God's cords always strengthen and stabilize.

But knots? They do the opposite. Knots diminish and destabilize.

A cord is woven with intention.
A knot is twisted by interruption.

A cord amplifies power.
A knot drains it.

A cord has structure.
A knot has confusion.

A cord is God-ordained.
A knot is enemy-manufactured.

God braids.
The enemy tangles.

A cord is covenant.
A knot is contamination.

This book, **INTO FREEDOM:** ***Reclaiming Your Authority From Spiritual Knots***, is the revelation of how to reverse contamination, confusion, spiritual crossing, and emotional tangling.

Knots work because they are subtle, hidden.

Now the serpent was more subtle than any of the beasts of the earth which the Lord God made. And he said to the woman: Why hath God commanded you, that you should not eat of every tree of paradise? (Genesis 3:1 DRB)

People think bondage is loud; it's usually not and that is how it is hidden for years, decades and even generations in a bloodline. They think spiritual warfare is dramatic; it doesn't have to be. Know this: some of the most spiritually dangerous things are quiet.

A knot forms when the enemy can't trap you outright —so he entangles you slowly, sneakily, quietly, subtly. Like a slithering, slimy, sauntering snake. The entanglement is not always obvious. Many times, it happens when you're having fun or when you're doing what everyone else is doing thinking, *"This is harmless."* It is not always with blatant sin, seduction, rebellion or temptation.

But, with just a thread of emotion or curiosity, or even loyalty, a person can be drawn and pulled into a knot. Notice what is drawn – your own humanity. The subtle serpent uses threads of your humanness to entrap.

With just a thread of concern, or an unfinished conversation, a wisp of spiritual energy or a thread of expectation or access – he gets in and attaches.

Knots do not begin with ropes; knots begin with threads. If enough threads gather — they braid into confusion.

THE SPIRIT REALM RECOGNIZES KNOTS EVEN WHEN YOU DON'T. Spiritual entanglements (knots) have signatures. They carry emotional pull, spiritual pressure, atmospheric disturbance, cognitive interference, energetic residue, discernment fog, and identity drift.

When you are knotted with someone, you begin to feel what they feel, sense what they sense, think about them unprovoked, is this not called obsession? You begin to carry weight that isn't yours, feel responsible for their emotions and filter decisions through their invisible presence. This is not love. This is not connection. This is not discernment. This is entanglement, and, it is not healthy.

An entanglement isn't a soul tie — it's an illegal knot. An entanglement ensnares. An entanglement holds with confusion. An entanglement weakens. It ropes in and ties up part of your humanity – even the good part and it makes you less functional as a human, less functional the way God intended you to function.

YOU CAN FEEL A KNOT, EVEN WHEN YOU CAN'T NAME IT. Knots communicate through sensation. Some may refer to it as a tightening in your spirit, an emotional pang, or a mental intrusion. Some report of a drained feeling after interacting and a sense of guilt when you pull back. There is a compulsive need to check on someone. Or, a strange fog comes over a person when their name comes up. There may be unexplained heaviness or the mind wanders to them at odd times.

There may be spiritual silence when dealing with them. Some experience internal alarms without logical reason. All this is the early language of entanglement.

A knot is forming. Once a knot forms, the enemy uses it to limit you. It may curtail your movement, or clarity. It may remove or erase your previously set boundaries, emotional autonomy, prophetic accuracy, and or spiritual authority.

Knots are spiritual constrictors. Like a snake.

Here's the revelation: What can be tangled can be untangled. What can be knotted can be unknotted. What can be braided can be unbraided.

This book teaches you how.

HOW DO I GET OUT OF THIS?

How do I break up with this knot?

No matter who or where or how ... this chapter can voice the frustration of all the things that will NOT get a person out of a knot. More than one knot can exist at once, so what is shared in this book must be applied for moving into freedom from entanglements.

We all know what stuck is. We know it's a knot. How do we break free or untangle the knot? What do *I* do?

First, if you lean to your understanding, you will not get out of it because your own understanding is what got you into it. Complaining about it won't get you out of it. Telling on the person you think caused it—because surely you didn't, will not get you out of it. Talking more, explaining or defending yourself because surely, it's not your fault. Trying harder is not the solution; the more you tug on a knot the tighter it becomes.

Just being patient and waiting will not get you out of a knot. Praying for the other person to change won't do it. Setting new boundaries or taking a break from the other person (if you even know who it is) doesn't solve it.

Just waiting it out, waiting for things to improve, or waiting for the other person to mature (grow up), won't do it. Being nicer won't get you out of it. Being quieter, more spiritual, such as giving an offering to make it break is not the answer. Praying and studying the Bible more, that's always advised, but it not the solution to untangling an entanglement, in and of itself. Read your Bible, because knowledge is deliverance but just hoping that it will 'fix' itself won't do it either. Acquiescing more will not loosen the knot; it is the catch.

None of these untie a knot; they only make it tighter.

Knots are not removed by effort. They are removed by separation. Separation is not negotiated; it is executed--, by God.

Well, have you considered how *many* knots you have? Or is this one the bane of your existence? Is this the one that finally made you notice that something is wrong?

People rarely have just one knot. They often have a family knot, relationship knot, a work knot, church knot, obligation knot, a social knot, and or a guilt knot. This could be why a person feels overwhelmed even if they are only recognizing one knot. You might not just be dealing with one knot. You could be dealing with a whole weave of knots--, like macrame' but not decorative or functional, instead they are functioning *against* you.

A person can be a natural knot-catcher, especially if they over-empathize, over-responsibilize, over-help, over-stay, or over-carry. That person may not mean to get entangled; they are simply very good at holding things for other people. You don't get entangled because you go looking for knots. Some people don't mean to get entangled. They are simply very good at holding things for other people.

Years ago, I taught a message called, *"Here, Hold My Jello."* Imagine someone handing you a pile of Jello — not in a bowl, not in a cup, just in your bare hands — and asking you to hold it for them. You try. You really do. You cup your hands, you steady yourself, you concentrate. Meanwhile, they are smiling, relaxed, going on with their life while you are struggling to keep something from slipping through your fingers that was never meant to be held that way. Nor was it your responsibility to hold it so they could be free.

That's how many entanglements begin.

Someone hands you their emotions, their worries, their fears, their instability, their confusion, their responsibilities, or their unresolved life. Because you are kind, capable, and caring, you try to hold it.

They feel relief; you feel pressure.

They walk lighter. You grow heavier. You're at home worried about a solution to fix their problems and they are out with friends having a good time. You may not even realize you've been handed something impossible to carry.

Knots often begin when you try to hold what was never yours to carry.

Some people don't look for knots. Knots look for them. You don't untie these knots; step away and let God unbraid it. Acquiescing more will not loosen the knot; it is the catch.

People assume that if they change to be better, kinder, nicer—a better Christian or more agreeable or more flexible that the tension will ease and maybe it will. But if the tension eases does that mean that your life begins to work again as it used to? Acquiescing, giving in is not relief--, well, not for you. It is still participation. Every time you yield to keep the peace, you add another turn to the braid.

You are not loosening anything. You are helping it hold. That is the catch.

Some women can be more vulnerable to this pattern — not because they're women, but because women are socialized to equate love with accommodation, patience, emotional labor, keeping the peace, and being that helpmeet--, being "supportive."

In this way, the behavior that tightens knots is often praised as virtue.

A person becomes susceptible to entanglement if they've been taught that their value is proven by how well they adjust to and 'get along with' other people. That type of message is given to women more often and earlier in life. When a relationship starts to feel off, often the go-to instinct for a woman is: try harder, be kinder, be more understanding, give more, or stay longer. Make it work. This is exactly what tightens the knot.

This is because of life conditioning.

Men can absolutely fall into this too, especially men who over-provide, over-rescue, over-tolerate, and equate love with sacrifice. Culturally, women are more often praised for "holding things together, even when what they're holding should be released.

Many women are especially vulnerable to entanglement, not because they are weak, but because they were taught that love looks like accommodation. The very qualities women are praised for, such as patience, support, and understanding, are the same qualities that make knots tighten when misapplied.

Who is praising that behavior? Maybe it's the entanglers.

ENTANGLEMENT NURSES

This might be the crux: those who also don't know it's an entanglement but they offer sincere "help" in the form of treating the symptoms without a real diagnosis. This keeps people stuck after the knot is already exposed.

It’s not that people don’t care, it’s that they don’t see what this is. So, they offer sincere help for the wrong problem. Many people will think this is a soul tie, but an entanglement is different than a soul tie.

These compassionate types that I will call Entanglement Nurses see sadness and say, “Cheer up” They see conflict and advise the person who is entangled to communicate better. When there is distance, the recommendation is, “try harder.” If they see exhaustion, they advise the person to “rest more.” When they see confusion you are encouraged, if not commanded to “pray more.” In all this, they are only treating symptoms.

The real issue is structural, but they don’t or can’t see that it’s a knot. It’s a knot.

No one can counsel a knot loose.

People around you may offer sincere help for a problem they do not recognize. They treat the symptoms because they cannot see the knot.

A person in a knot may say of even well-meaning folks, “I asked for help, and all the help I received made me feel worse.” That’s not because the advice was bad in general, but because it was wrong for that particular situation.

“Why didn’t anyone help me get out of this?”

Because they didn’t know what they were looking at.

Even true friends will have a brand of comfort that sounds something like this: “He's a bad boyfriend; break up with him."

That might be true; he might be a bad boyfriend, or friend, or acquaintance or co-worker, or church member. But that doesn’t solve the knot in and of itself.

So, you break up with them. Now there's a residual undealt with knot and or soul tie and the person is marching into a new relationship with those **same** spiritual issues, relationship defects, and baggage and there you go. Layer upon layer, thread upon thread, cord upon cord.

Suddenly she's 30 and where's her husband?

Sometimes the advice really is as simple as, “This relationship isn’t healthy — step away.” That can be wise.

The problem is what happens after the step away if no one helps the person process what the connection did to them.

So the sequence looks like this:

- Relationship ends.
- Everyone exhales: "Good. That's over."
- No one asks what habits, beliefs, or roles formed during it.

The person carries those beliefs forward, not because they're careless, because they were never shown how to examine the residue. Ending the relationship removes the person. It does not automatically remove the patterns formed inside it.

Over time, if this happens repeatedly, people can feel layered carrying expectations they didn't choose. reacting from old roles (they will call this baggage. Comparing new people to old dynamics. wondering why the same types of situations reappear.

They start to ask painful questions about themselves and their future. It's not that you're broken. It's that you were never shown how to clear what was left behind.

Breaking up can end a relationship. It does not always end the imprint that relationship left on you.

KNOTS UPON KNOTS

A person you may go to for help -- a person, not a business-- that person gets you to or lets you tell ALL your business as to why you need this help and then they say, No. Now they know your vulnerability or need.

That experience is a power imbalance moment. You open yourself. You explain everything. You expose need. And then the person says, "No." Now they have your story, your weakness, your timing, your urgency. You leave with nothing resolved, and your vulnerability exposed. That can feel like humiliation, exploitation, regret, and self-blame.

It can create a new micro-knot if you're thinking such as, "I shouldn't have said all that." Knots tighten when vulnerability is mishandled. When someone is entangled, they are more likely to over-disclose, over-explain, over-trust, over-seek validation. Not everyone is safe.

Not everyone who listens is equipped to hold what you share. When you are trying to get free, you may reach for help. But not every listener is a lifeline. Some will let you pour out everything and then step back. Now they know your vulnerability, and you are left exposed. Reaching freedom from entanglements requires discernment about where you place your story.

Vulnerability is not weakness. but vulnerability without discernment can create new knots. This is not about fear. It's about governance.

Knots Upon Knots speaks of accumulated entanglement, compounded weight, layers, repetition, generational patterns, unfinished endings, and stacking. It carries gravity.

Knots upon knots is w*hen you didn't just untie one thing.*

Unresolved residue from past relationships tends to build up over time, layering itself beneath the surface and coloring future interactions. When endings are not fully processed—when emotional or spiritual ties are left unaddressed—these residues remain, quietly influencing how we connect, trust, and respond. Simply ending a relationship at the surface level, or making a "symptom-level exit," does not always sever the deeper, structural bonds that were formed. These structural ties can persist, keeping us bound to old patterns and unhealed experiences even as we attempt to move forward.

As a result, with each new relationship, a person may feel increasingly entangled. Frustrated. Trying harder and harder to please the person they are with. That means going for things they shouldn't agree with. It could mean shrinking. It could mean being controlled because you want to please this person because you don't want them to leave you.

It's shameful, really; you don't want the shame of losing another relationship, not even evaluating if it is a relationship you should try to hold on to. Not even seeing how you are contorting and distorting yourself to stay in it. To stay in what? To stay in the knot.

Contorting and distorting yourself will surely put you in and keep you in a knot. That's what a knot it; when someone has you tied down.

Rather than starting anew, the weight and complexity of previous knots are carried into the present, making each subsequent connection more complicated to navigate. This accumulation of unresolved issues can lead to a sense of being "tied up" or overwhelmed, even in situations that might otherwise be simple or straightforward.

Moreover, the tendency to "move on" without intentionally clearing these lingering cords only multiplies the complexity. Each time we bypass the work of genuine closure—failing to release emotional, psychological, or spiritual agreements—we add another layer to the tangle. Over time, these patterns compound, making liberation and authentic new beginnings increasingly difficult. It becomes essential, then, to not only leave situations physically but to withdraw our energy, intention, and consent fully, ensuring that the knots of the past are not simply hidden, but actually untied.

You thought you were starting over. You were actually layering over. This focuses on multiple ties at once, overlapping roles, and repeating patterns.

Simple breakups don't always clear cords. Residue, like iniquity travels forward.

People rarely suffer from one knot. They suffer from unfinished endings, unexamined residue, and unwithdrawn agreements. Learn how to leave a room. When you are finished with a thing, especially something that has depleted you because of its spiritual implications, you must back out of it completely. Don't just leave physically.

This becomes layer upon layer, thread upon thread, and cord upon cord. Someone who tends to the wounded, stabilizes chaos, comforts instability, and manages other people's emotional emergencies are very prone to this. It does so almost automatically.

Some people are not looking for trouble. They are looking for people to help, but without discernment, helping becomes entering. Entering becomes holding. Holding becomes binding. Because they are good at stabilizing unstable people, unstable people find them. It's not that you are a magnet for that type, it's that they are looking for you and types like you. Don't be so prideful; if it is not you, it will be someone nearly like you. Unstable people may be finding you, and it's not you who is finding them. Still, that's how repetition happens.

Not because a person like you is foolish, but because you are predictable in your kindness.

A person without relational discernment may not recognize a knot until they are already holding it. Without discernment, compassion becomes access. Without awareness, a person can feel "completely tied."

Not because one catastrophic event happened but because they never closed loops. They never withdrew misplaced responsibility. They never stopped catching falling people, layer upon layer. Structurally, Entanglement Nurses explains the helper personality.

The "gift of helps," as referenced in the Bible (1 Corinthians 12:28), is a real and desired gift to have. This gift describes people uniquely equipped to support, serve, and uplift others. They often work behind the scenes to address needs and stabilize situations. This is the type of person who will do some or all the work and let the other person take all the credit and the glory for that stellar work. This helper may think they are sowing into a relationship.

What relationship the taker may be thinking? I'm wonderful and I deserve this help. People are always helping me; you're not special. However, here's something else you can help me with. The cycle repeats into entanglement, if that helps gift is not governed. This will repeat until the “helper” decides to get free from entanglement.

This spiritual gift of helps is marked by compassion, willingness to assist, and sensitivity to the burdens of others. In the context of this book, the gift of helps can be seen as both a blessing and a challenge. Those with this gift may instinctively tend to the wounded, manage chaos, and comfort instability, as described in the preceding chapter, "Entanglement Nurses."

Without discernment and healthy boundaries, their kindness and predictability can lead to repeated patterns of entanglement. The biblical call to serve others is noble, but it is important to withdraw unsanctioned or misplaced responsibility and untangle past agreements to avoid being "tied up" by unresolved emotional and spiritual cords. In this way, the gift of helps, when practiced with Wisdom, can be a source of healing and liberation, rather than a cycle of overwhelm and unfinished endings.

When someone is struggling with emotional or spiritual challenges, they are often drawn to share their struggles with a person who possesses the Biblical counseling gift, which is sometimes referred to as the gift of Wisdom, discernment, or exhortation (Romans 12:8, 1 Corinthians 12:8-10). Unlike confiding in just anyone, approaching someone with this spiritual gift brings a sense of safety, understanding, and genuine guidance. The individual with a counseling gift listens with empathy, offers insight rooted in compassion and scriptural Wisdom, and is less likely to judge or dismiss the depth of the concern. Those with this gift in earnest will not disclose what was discussed in the counseling session; they are discreet to the utmost. Their presence can feel stabilizing, and their words often carry a healing or clarifying effect, helping the person untangle complex emotions and find constructive paths forward.

In contrast, sharing sensitive issues with someone who does not possess this gift may result in well-meaning but unfiltered advice, lack of true understanding, or even inadvertent harm if the listener is unprepared for the emotional weight involved. If you hear your business in the streets, see it online, or it is on blast in the family group chat or announced in the church prayer meeting, then you will then know you weren't talking to someone with the Counseling Gift.

That's painful. Sorry.

The Biblical counseling gift makes a person approachable for deep matters, as others sense their capacity for discernment, confidentiality, and spiritual support. This distinction explains why people often seek out those with this gift during times of crisis or confusion, desiring not just to be heard, but also to be guided toward healing and resolution.

Knots Upon Knots explains the cumulative effect. Babs seems to have a problem in life—well, nearly every problem. She has issues with family, friends, co-workers. romantic interests. EVERYONE seems to want to mistreat her or be a dramatic problem to her. Recently it was the sister of the guy she was seeing, and she had never even met the sister. (It's a lot.)

When it feels like everyone around someone becomes a dramatic problem — family, friends, co-workers, romantic partners, even people they've barely met, it is statistically unlikely that *everyone* someone meets is uniquely dramatic. Concerning spiritual matters and on deliverance ground there could be a *spirit of reproach* on this person and she has a spirit of rejection that makes her react to their reaction to her.

When a pattern repeats, we look at the environments they enter, the traits they are drawn to, the boundaries they set (or don't set), the roles they assume, what behavior they tolerate. Patterns don't usually mean "magnetism." They usually mean selection + tolerance + reinforcement.

There are a few common dynamics behind this. It could be that high drama feels familiar to Babs. If someone grew up around instability, chaos can feel normal. Calm can feel boring, so they unconsciously choose high-intensity people.

It could be that she is the one who is high intensity, so she finds people who have rescuer wiring. Some people are wired to stabilize others. They attract people who need stabilizing. Babs could benefit from emotional stabilization.

Predatory or chaotic personalities scan for over-explainers, over-givers, quick trusters, those who appear desperate, and conflict-avoiders. These people seem to have no boundaries or weak boundaries so they can attract the gamut.

The low discernment + high empathy types attract a certain type. That combination is powerful — and risky. *Why do I attract this kind over and over? Do I have a target on my back?* (Of course, you do not.) They are repeatedly stepping into dynamics they don't yet recognize. There's hope though; that's trainable and correctable.

When discernment is underdeveloped and compassion is overdeveloped, chaos will feel invited. If drama follows someone everywhere, it doesn't automatically mean they are bad, but it does mean something in their selection or response system is unexamined.

It's usually one (or more) of these dynamics:

Pattern Selection. People don't randomly meet chaotic personalities at higher rates than everyone else. They may consistently choose high-intensity partners. They may have been born into and stay in unstable family systems. They may tolerate boundary crossings. They may be the type to overlook early red flags. They could respond to drama instead of stepping away. Over time it *looks* like "everyone is dramatic." It's often the same type in different bodies.

They say that God will send you the same test over and again until you *get it.*

Some people interpret neutral or minor conflict as major betrayal. If someone's internal lens is, "People mistreat me. They will scan for confirming evidence. This isn't lying, it's cognitive filtering.

Role Reinforcement. If someone repeatedly plays:

- The Victim
- The Rescuer
- The Target
- The Misunderstood One

Other people subconsciously step into complementary roles. Drama requires participation--, everyone playing their part--, over and over again.

Babs may find herself in high reactivity environments. If she reacts strongly, talks extensively, processes publicly, or loops others into conflict, drama grows legs. Conflict that could die quietly becomes oxygenated. Now, about the sister of the guy she was seeing — someone she never even met.

When third-party drama enters quickly, it usually means: The man himself is unstable or conflict-prone. He triangulates. Or she is hyper-alert to perceived rejection. It doesn't mean she's cursed but it could look like it. Still, there is no reason not to pray fervently. Praying a prayer you don't need will never hurt you, while not praying a prayer you need can be devastating. She may not be cursed, but it could mean that something about her relationship ecosystem is chaotic.

If drama follows someone everywhere, like a cartoon character with a rain cloud over his head, one of three things is true: They repeatedly choose unstable people. They lack firm boundaries. They interpret friction as persecution. Sometimes, it's all three.

If conflict surrounds you in every environment, it is time to examine your selection patterns and your tolerance thresholds. When chaos is everywhere, the common denominator is not fate; it's pattern that can be clearly seen.

The core wound, the first untied knot, say in family or childhood, structurally pre-writes some people for problems. The first untied knot, especially one formed in childhood or family, often becomes a template for things to come for that person.

If a child grows up inside a knot, meaning roles are blurred, emotions are unmanaged and boundaries are weak. It could be that responsibility is misplaced. Love is conditional or unstable.

What happens?

The child adapts. Adaptation becomes normal. Normal becomes identity. Identity becomes expectation. Expectation becomes selection. Selection becomes repetition.

No one decides this consciously. It just feels familiar.

The first knot can quietly pre-write later problems because it defines what feels "normal" and what feels like love. what feels like responsibility, what feels like safety, and what feels like intensity. If intensity = connection in childhood. Calm can feel like emptiness in adulthood.

If over-functioning = love in childhood, then rescuing can feel *romantic* later. If walking on eggshells = peace in childhood, that person will tolerate instability longer than others. This doesn't mean someone is doomed, it means they are operating on early programming.

Once that first knot is seen and untied, the template loses power. That's why this book, **INTO FREEDOM** matters so much, because until the original framework is examined, a person thinks, "Why does this keep happening?"

After it's examined, they say, "Oh. I've been replaying something. The first knot does not determine your future, but it often teaches you what feels familiar enough to repeat.

Now, let's get out of all these knots.

THE 7 DIMENSIONS OF UNBRAIDING

Unbraiding is not a single moment. It is not a one-sentence prayer. It is not a quick emotional release. Unbraiding is dimensional. Just like entanglements weave through layers of your inner world, deliverance must unwind through those same layers.

Knots don't form in one place. They form in multiple dimensions — mind, emotions, atmosphere, identity, assignment, dreams, and the inner court. So, unbraiding must match the depth of the entanglement.

This chapter reveals the 7 Dimensions of Unbraiding. This will be a surgical process God uses to loosen every thread of entanglement. This is the part that can set you FREE.

Dimensions of unbraiding will show up in the natural as: separation; moving both or one. the other person just poof goes away -- even ghosting. Rarely do you remain best friends after an entanglement is exposed and undone.

The Dimensions of Unbraiding show up in very ordinary, very visible ways.

How Unbraiding Appears in Real Life

When cords are cut in the unseen, the first evidence is usually seen in the natural. It looks like distance, separation, relocation, silence, access ending, communication stopping, routines breaking, and roles dissolving.

Sometimes one person moves. Sometimes both do. Sometimes the other person simply disappears from your life without drama or explanation. Sometimes it looks like ghosting. Not because someone is cruel, but because the connection that sustained the relationship is no longer there.

You rarely remain "best friends" because once the entanglement is exposed and undone, you see clearly how much was obligation, how much was imbalance, how much was role confusion, how much was emotional labor, how little was actually mutual. You cannot "go back" to the previous dynamic because you now understand what it was.

Clarity changes posture. When God unbraids cords in the spirit, the evidence often appears as very ordinary separation in the natural. Unbraiding rarely looks dramatic. It usually looks like distance.

"Oh. That's why this relationship just… stopped." Not because something failed but because something finished.

DIMENSION 1 — UNBRAIDING THE MIND

Your mind must be untangled from the loop. Free your mind, and the rest will follow. The first dimension of the knot is always cognitive. Signs your mind is entangled are if you are having intrusive thoughts, emotional replay, mental noise around one person. If you are imagining, rehearsing, mentally repeating conversations, especially with over analysis you need to be unknotted or unbraided to this person or situation. If you are in rumination, inner turmoil, hesitation, or mental fog, your mind needs to be unbraided.

Unbraiding the mind requires:

Pull the thought back into your ownership. Say, *That is not my thought. That is not my emotional debt.*

Sever the cognitive loop. Replace the mental loop with a single grounding truth. "He is not my assignment." "She is not my lane." "This is not covenant." "This is not clarity." "This knot is not mine."

Restore the mental silence. Once the mental thread is pulled, your mind will feel quieter. This is the first loosening.

DIMENSION 2 — UNBRAIDING THE EMOTIONS

You must reclaim emotional sovereignty. You cannot unbraid a knot while emotionally entangled. This dimension targets emotional dependency, guilt, longing, misplaced compassion, emotional responsibility, sensitivity to their mood, emotional absorption. Unbraiding the emotions requires emotional sovereignty.

Emotional Sovereignty Statement: "My emotions do not belong to this connection. Next be sure to s**eparate their emotions from your own.** Ask yourself, "What part of this feeling is ME, and what part is THEM?"

Reclaim Your Emotional Center. Place your hand over your chest and declare: "I return to myself." When the emotional strand loosens, the knot loses power.

DIMENSION 3 — UNBRAIDING THE ATMOSPHERE. *Their atmosphere must leave your atmosphere.*

This is where many Christians do not realize they're entangled. Entanglement carries atmospheric residue: heaviness, fog, influence, pressure, spiritual noise, lingering energy, and emotional weight.

When someone leaves a mark on your atmosphere, your peace becomes destabilized. Unbraiding the atmosphere requires **revoking Atmospheric Permission.** Do that first. Say, "I remove your atmosphere from my space."

Next, breaking Spiritual Residue

Open a window. Light fills the room. Pray, "Peace, return to my environment." Now, restore i**nternal**

airflow. As the atmosphere clears, your body will feel lighter. This is not emotional; this is spiritual and that act was prophetic.

DIMENSION 4 — UNBRAIDING THE IDENTITY

This is the dimension where the damage went deepest.

Identity entanglements change the way you see: yourself, your worth, your voice, your role and your assignment, expectations and limits. When your identity shifts around one person, your soul has been tied into their presence.

Unbraiding the identity requires a few steps. First, there must be **Identity Recalibration:**

Speak your true name: "I am [your name]. I am not theirs. I am not defined by them." You must mean this. Speak it over and again until you get release.

Next, re-seating Yourself in Your Inner Court. Picture your spirit sitting back on the throne of your identity. Now, reclaiming Your Internal Authority from this person, idol, entity -- by declaring, "I reclaim my authority over my life."

This is the dimension that restores your spine — spiritual, emotional, and internal. You are in Christ, so you can give authority to Christ. Be sure Christ is seated on the Throne of your heart. Amen.

DIMENSION 5 — UNBRAIDING THE ASSIGNMENT

You must separate your calling from their influence

This is crucial. Assignment entanglements are how people derail destinies. When a person gets tied into your calling, you begin to question your direction, delay your purpose, adjust your pace, worry about their reactions, filter your decisions through their invisible presence.

Unbraiding the assignment requires that you return not your own lane. Say aloud: "I return to my lane." Add to it and there is no other person in my lane or steering me or my vehicle of destiny. Just me. Better: Just me and the Lord. (Jesus take the wheel).

Disentangling the Purpose Thread. say, "My assignment is not connected to them. There assignment is not connected to me."

Reclaim Your Future. "This connection has no jurisdiction over my destiny." When this dimension unbraids, you feel momentum return.

DIMENSION 6 — UNBRAIDING THE DREAM REALM

Dream access is a sign of spiritual entanglement.

When someone shows up in your dreams uninvited, repeatedly, emotionally charged, symbolically, intrusively, atmospherically, …it means a spiritual thread has entered your subconscious gate. When people follow you into your dream realm, that is a boundary crossed. It is too far. Your dreams are a sacred space.

Unbraiding the dream realm requires:

A. Closing the Dream Gate

Say, "Every unauthorized presence in my dreams — leave, in the Name of Jesus."

B. Cutting Dream Cords

"My dreams belong to God, not to this connection."

C. Reclaiming the Night Realm

"No more intrusion.
No more influence.
No more entry."

Once this thread loosens, sleep becomes peaceful again.

DIMENSION 7 — UNBRAIDING THE INNER COURT.

This is the final and deepest level of unbraiding.

Your inner court is your emotional temple. It is your spiritual home. It is your identity throne and your prophetic center. Your inner court is your decision-making chamber. It is your seat of Peace.

Entanglement gives someone a seat they were never invited to.

Unbraiding the inner court requires:

A. Eviction

"I remove you from my inner court, in the Name of Jesus."

B. Resetting the Throne

"My spirit belongs to God alone, in Jesus' Name."

C. Re-establishing Divine Order

"I restore divine sovereignty over my temple in the Name of Jesus."

This final dimension is where everything comes back into alignment. Once the inner court is clear, the knot is broken. This is the true liberation moment.

THE PROPHECY OF THE 7 DIMENSIONS

God unbraids the same way knots formed — in layers, in dimensions, in threads. This is why some people feel better after a closure conversation but still feel "off" spiritually… The knot wasn't emotional. It was dimensional.

And now — you know how to unwind every layer.

DECLARATION:

"I unbraid my mind.
I unbraid my emotions.
I unbraid my atmosphere.
I unbraid my identity.
I unbraid my assignment.
I unbraid my dreams.
I unbraid my inner court.
Nothing remains tied.
Nothing remains tangled.
I return to myself

in the Name of Jesus."

THE UNBRAIDING ANGEL

Many people think spiritual freedom requires intensity. They think deliverance must be loud, dramatic. Chaotic. Violent. Sudden. But there is another dimension of deliverance. It can be gentle, surgical, precise, silent, and holy.

Next we will discuss the ministry of the Unbraiding Angel. THE UNBRAIDING ANGEL is an angelic operation assigned by God to loosen, unravel, untie, unweave, cut, unwind, separate, disentangle every knot in the soul, spirit, mind, atmosphere, and assignment of a believer. This is not fiction; this is Scripture, activated. The Unbraiding Angel bypasses human consent rituals, operates on God's timing, overrides emotional attachment, protects the innocent even when the innocent is still *"goo-gaw"* over the other person involved in the entanglement.

When an innocent is protected by God from an overbearing type and maybe the innocent (she) is still all *goo gaw* over the controlling, overbearing, destabilizing guy and he's a whole problem, God gets him out of the picture, fast, decisively, quickly. But she's stuck, lamenting, oh, she misses him so much. Dear Reader: God does not ask for our preferred method of removal or breaking an entanglement. First of all, He's not our butler.

Entanglements persist because access was granted. proximity was tolerated. ambiguity was allowed. control was retained. If God were to free someone *while preserving their sense of control*, the entanglement would simply re-form.

So, Scripture shows a consistent pattern: God removes people from situations in ways that prevent return. That often feels abrupt, final, inconvenient, or even embarrassing.

But it is **merciful**. This is not punishment. This is protective extraction. God removes *him* before she is ready because her discernment has not yet caught up to her affection. Affection forms faster than Wisdom. God does not wait for affection to resolve itself when harm is imminent. So, He intervenes upstream.

This is the same pattern seen with:

Hagar removed from abuse.

Israel removed from Pharaoh.

David removed from Saul.

Joseph removed from Potiphar's house.

Jesus was very discerning, but He was removed from crowds that wanted to seize Him prematurely.

In these cases, God acts before the person emotionally agrees.

The lovestruck person may feel grief instead of relief because what she lost was the *feeling,* the *fantasy,* the *potential,* the *version of him she hoped was real,* not the man as he actually was. That grief is real, but it does **not** mean the removal was wrong. God does not make mistakes.

God will often remove what you cannot yet release — because waiting for clarity would cost you safety. Sometimes the Mercy is not that you see clearly — but that the danger is removed before you must.

This happens most often with overbearing types. Overbearing personalities escalate quickly, collapse boundaries, interpret affection as entitlement, punish hesitation, intensify control when they sense attachment.

If God waited for her to "fall out of love," she would already be entangled more deeply. So, He shortens the timeline.

The separation feels unfair *at first b*ecause she experiences loss without explanation, grief without closure, confusion without context. That's why *Into Freedom* matters, it provides retrospective understanding. Freedom often makes sense **after** distance is established, not before.

Missing someone is not evidence they were safe or would ever change, or ever be good for you.

Grief is not proof of error. Sometimes grief is simply the cost of being spared.

The overbearing is the predator type. They are dangerous because they are relationally aggressive and psychologically invasive. They often have no bounds and no stops.

Key traits:

- **Accelerated attachment** – they move fast, press closeness early
- **Entitlement to access** – your attention feels *owed* to them
- **Boundary override** – "no" is treated as confusion, or a challenge, not refusal
- **Emotional intensity** – charm mixed with urgency
- **Interpretation of affection as permission**
- **Possessive framing** – "we," "us," "meant to be," before agreement

They do not wait to be chosen. They **assume the bond**. That's the predatory element.

God removes *them* quickly

Because these personalities:

- escalate when attachment exists
- punish hesitation

- collapse autonomy
- tighten control when they sense affection

If the innocent person remains emotionally soft while proximity continues, the situation **will not self-correct**.

So, God acts decisively; He is our Protector. He cuts that person's access to you. Communication ends. Distance is enforced and circumstances are altered. All this is not because she was wrong, but because at that time she may have been distracted, unguarded, or outmatched physically or spiritually. Yes, that predator may have stepped to her with a dark anointing that she never suspected. She has set down her own discernment and instead of getting out of Dodge, she walks right into it because she is being spiritually drawn.

But she may think it's just attraction; they are drawn to one another. No.

She grieves and may even cry out to God to restore the connection (that she thinks is a relationship) all the while God is the one who removed it. Just because she is crying, even though God hears that does not invalidate the removal of a predator. She thinks she likes guys like that, daring, exciting, rule breakers, never reaching for the word, predator. He's a predator and predators look for prey.

Still, she is mourning the fantasy, the potential, the feeling of being chosen, the version of him she believed in. She is mourning what she feels is loss. Saints of God can we not all see that the devil can turn himself into an angel of light? Can we not see that temptations are temptations because they tempt. Can we not see that the bait the devil puts out is bait because people want it? Can we not see that what the enemy has can both look and feel good?

Discern every spirit.

This person is **not** mourning safety. She is actually mourning the loss of a temptation and she won, she actually won, but doesn't realize it yet.

Go ahead and grieve until clarity is reached. Grief is simply the nervous system catching up to protection. We should know that God is good. God is always good. God is our Protector and He is always doing things for our good and for our benefit. Feels like? What it feels like? How are your carnal senses supposed to understand the acts of God?

God will remove a predator before affection matures into captivity. When someone is still emotionally open, God may act externally to do what discernment has not yet done internally.

Hopefully we can just ask God about a thing instead of perpetually mourning or waiting until you find out what this predator did to someone else and finally you see and you're glad it's not you.

The fact that he needed or used entanglement meant that he couldn't go the usual route because his motives were not clean.

> Verily, verily, I say unto you, He that entereth not by the door into the sheepfold, but climbeth up some other way, the same is a thief and a robber. (John 10:1)

Entanglement is not the door to covenant. A thief doesn't use the door; he may use a window or some other access point.

God is working for our good; sometimes the Mercy is interruption of a thing that looks good, sounds good, and even smells good- today. But it is a pit dug for you for later on.

God will remove a predator...

- **"God will remove a predator before affection matures into captivity."**
- **"God will remove a predator even when the heart has not caught up to the danger."**
- **"God removes predators early, because love should never require survival."**
- **"When discernment is still forming, God acts first."** (softer, still firm)

Please know, not every man is a villain; most are not. No every woman is immature or silly. This chapter is about the Mercy of God.

How God breaks you out of an entanglement knot even before you realize it's a knot or start praying for it is uniquely up to God. Should a person who is praying to be 'busted out of' an entanglement be surprised when they don't have 'control' of HOW God may break it up? when God separates, He REALLY separates)

Biblical pattern: when God separates, He separates hard. We've already mentioned a few examples.

God does not loosen entanglements. He breaks access points.

People feel "out of control" during the break because entanglements falsely give the illusion of:

- predictability
- influence
- emotional leverage
- negotiated outcomes

Freedom removes those illusions. So, what remains is distance, silence, reordering, and unfamiliar territory. That may feel like loss, when it's gain. When you pray to be freed, you are surrendering the method as well as the outcome. God does not untangle by consultation.

Freedom is rarely achieved with permission from what held you.

God's separations feel "extreme" because partial separations: invite reattachment, preserve emotional hooks, allow narrative rewriting. God separates far enough that the old pattern cannot resume. That's not punishment. That's protection.

People who want freedom but insist on controlling the process are usually still negotiating with the entanglement. Once the prayer becomes sincere, the loss of control is not a failure; it's the confirmation. Lack of control is often the evidence that the prayer was actually answered.

When praying for release from the overbearing type, the oppressive types, the control will be lost the most dramatically.

When God intervenes to free someone from an entanglement, those who benefited from the entanglement are the ones most destabilized. That's not accidental. Overbearing types rely on proximity, access, predictability, emotional leverage, and assumed authority. When God breaks an entanglement, He removes the conditions that made their dominance possible. They don't just lose the person — they lose the *system.*

Separation feels "extreme" in these cases. For oppressive personalities mild distance doesn't work, polite boundaries are ignored, clarification is treated as negotiation, kindness is interpreted as permission. So, God does not trim the connection. He ends the access.

That's why relocations happen. roles collapse. alliances dissolve. platforms shift; communication ends abruptly. Not as punishment — but as containment.

When freedom threatens an oppressor, God does not negotiate terms. He removes reach. God separates most decisively where control has been most abused.

This is especially true for the innocent or immature. The innocent and immature cannot yet recognize manipulation early, enforce boundaries consistently, or withstand pressure without self-doubt

God intervenes **externally** when internal defenses are not yet formed. That's protection, not infantilization.

Scripture shows this again and again:

- God moves the vulnerable *out* of reach
- then teaches them governance later

Freedom first. Maturity second. God will grow you up after He gets you out of harm's way.

The Governing Principle (Biblical + experiential): When a person prays to be *freed* from an entanglement, they are not asking God to optimize the situation — they are asking Him to end it.

Divine endings are not negotiated.

When teaching the Disciples to pray, didn't Jesus say, Let it be done. There you go; it is simply done. God is decisive, especially in areas of safety or danger.

That's Divine intervention. Unbraiding is an angelic process, and it is not something that we can control. If we could control it, then why and how did it happen in the first place?

They can't. I kinda bet you already knew that.

THE BIBLICAL PATTERN OF ANGELIC UNTYING

Every major deliverance moment in Scripture includes an Angel:

1. **Peter's Chains -** *Acts 12:7–9*
   An Angel **loosed** the chains; he did not break them. It was loosed, that is, untied.

2. Daniel in the Lions' Den

An Angel **shut** the lions' mouths. Shutting a mouth is undoing the threat. It is loosening danger.

3. Lazarus's Grave Clothes - John 11:44
Jesus resurrected Lazarus— but **men unwrapped him**, demonstrating dual roles:

- God breaks Death
- Angels and humans **untie bondage**

4. Isaiah 58:6

To loose the bands of wickedness… to undo heavy burdens… to let the oppressed go free… and to break every yoke.

Loose = unbraid.
Undo = unweave.
Break = end the authority.

This is not just metaphor; this is instruction. There must be a **loosing** before there is a **breaking**. Breaking without unbraiding causes internal damage. Unbraiding is humane, holy, and healing.

THE UNBRAIDING ANGEL OPERATES IN THREE WAYS

The Unbraiding Angel performs **three** silent operations:

1. THE LOOSENING

The angel gently unties the spiritual knot.

Signs this is happening:

- you feel "lighter" suddenly
- you stop thinking about the person involuntarily
- their emotional gravity breaks
- the knot's tension loosens
- guilt evaporates

- internal pressure lifts
- you feel oxygen in your spirit
- the connection loses its charge

This is not emotional. This is spiritual surgery.

2. THE DETANGLING

The angel separates the threads — one dimension at a time. This is when the 7 dimensions begin breaking off.

Thoughts settle. Emotions regulate. Atmosphere clears. Identity stabilizes. Dreams normalize. Your inner court empties. Your assignment becomes clearer.

Signs:

- relief
- restored focus
- prophetic accuracy returns
- you stop "feeling" their emotions
- no more internal turbulence
- peace reappears without effort

This is the ministry of the Unbraiding Angel.

3. THE SEVERING

The final spiritual thread is cut.

This is the moment you feel:

- closure without conversation
- release without confrontation
- peace without understanding
- distance without conflict
- neutrality without resentment
- stillness without explanation

This is when the knot is officially dissolved. There is no fight. No panic. No collapse. No drama. Just a clean break.

The enemy knots. God severs. But only after He unbraids.

THE CHARACTER OF THE UNBRAIDING ANGEL

This Angel is gentle, quiet, dignified, surgical, immaculate, respectful, holy, precise. It does not rip, tear, or yank. It loosens, unwinds, and frees.

It respects the soul. It respects the mind. It respects the emotional integrity of the believer. This is your angelic assistance. Enjoy the Peace.

INTO FREEDOM

On the day you were born your cord was not cut, nor were you washed with water to make you clean, nor were you rubbed with salt or wrapped in cloths.
(Ezekiel 16:4)

This verse speaks of uncut attachment. This verse is foundational

1. *The cord not being cut* = entanglement at origin. Before there is:

- rebellion
- sin
- behavior, or
- choice

there was a failure of separation at the birth of the subject of that verse. An uncut cord means that life is received, but independence is not granted. It means that nourishment exists, but governance does not. It also means that survival happens without proper transition

That is the root of entanglements. You see then, it is not because of ignorance or wickedness, necessarily, but there was *no clean severing.*

If we come into the world seemingly unwanted, uncared for, unprotected, (untreated) we may appear then to be more susceptible to becoming entangled. People who are wanted, cared for, protected, emotionally regulated, and properly bounded are **less vulnerable** to unhealthy entanglements. They are less vulnerable, but not immune. A person could grow up feeling chosen instead of tolerated, safe instead of anxious, seeing boundaries modeled, and learning that love doesn't require over-functioning. In this case they would develop internal stability, clearer red-flag detection, less tolerance for foolishness and chaos, and have less of a need to rescue.

That would reduce susceptibility, but even well-tended people can misread chemistry. They can underestimate manipulation--, they are not even programmed to see manipulation. They didn't grow up with anything like that. They can overestimate their own ability to help. They could meet someone unusually skilled at destabilizing, and still fall into entanglements.

Knots feed on hunger for affirmation, fear of abandonment, overdeveloped sense of responsibility, and blurred or non-existent boundaries

Proper tending strengthens discernment, but even the well-raised must still choose wisely in adulthood.

We are to be in the world, but not *of* it. So, when we come into the world, even as we have been conceived in sin and born into iniquity, we come out from among them (the world) and we are washed by the washing of the water of the Word. We are cut from the desires of the world, and we receive legitimacy in Christ.

We are not supposed to have worldly entanglements and anyone who wants to entangle you, as we have discussed, is not entering into your life the correct way or bonding with you the proper way.

Come out from among them. In the world while all the while not of it. Upbringing shapes susceptibility; it does not remove agency. Others influence us. They do not control our adult choices. We are formed by family, culture, church, and our own experiences. But we are not frozen by them; we are not set in stone. We live and move and have being and make decisions all day every day.

I must own my own choices. And that is based on what I was taught, what I internalized, and what I chose to ignore, tolerate, or continue. I cannot just blame others for knots or disruptions in life.

Your upbringing may explain your patterns. It does not excuse your continuation of them. Formation influences you. It does not absolve you.

Everything is not your fault. Yes, you were shaped by others, but you are responsible for what you maintain as an adult.

2. Washing, salting, swaddling are rightful authority actions. The cutting of the cord, the salting, the swaddling are not cosmetic. Being washed, and cleansed speaks of legitimacy.

Salted speaks of covenant preservation, value, worth. Wrapped, means covering, identity, and belonging.

> Ye are the salt of the earth: but if the salt have lost his savour, wherewith shall it be salted? it is thenceforth good for nothing, but to be cast out, and to be trodden under foot of men.(Matthew 5:13)

When authority fails to do this the person grows but never fully *arrives.* That produces adults who are spiritually alive, emotionally bound, and possibly relationally tethered. You need to be a free, whole person to finish your work here on Earth. That does not mean unmarried or free from people, it means untied, unknotted, unentangled, unowned. You need to be a whole soul possessing your vessel in sanctification and honor.

3. Freedom assumes:

- the cord *can* be cut
- someone has the right to cut it
- the person can survive the separation

Authority answers the questions: *Who was supposed to cut the cord — and what happens when they didn't?* Until that is named, freedom feels like abandonment. separation feels like death. deliverance feels cruel

4. This verse also reframes the Unbraiding Angel. Unbraiding is not punishment. It is **delayed midwifery**. It is God doing *later* what should have been done earlier.

That's why it feels sudden, it feels forceful, it feels final. it is not violence. It is necessary severing for life to continue.

5. This verse brings Peace instead of heaviness. Ezekiel 16 does not start with accusation. It starts with context. God says, in essence, *"Before I address what you became, let Me tell you what was not done for you."*

That is Mercy.

HOW TO RECOGNIZE THE UNBRAIDING ANGEL AT WORK

You know this Angel is present when: Something lifts without reason. You didn't pray hard. You didn't cry. You didn't argue. You didn't confront. But the weight is gone.

You lose interest without bitterness. The emotional "charge" disappears. The attachment dissolves. The urgency stops. You feel mentally quiet. The noise leaves. The mental loop stops. The rehearsing ends.

Dreams intrusion stops immediately. Night disturbance lifts. Sleep becomes peaceful.

Your discernment returns. Your vision sharpens. Your intuition reactivates. Your spirit feels "yours" again. You feel "right-sized" again. Your identity returns. Your internal authority rises. Your emotional sovereignty resets.

PART III
THE MOMENT OF SEVERING

There comes a point when understanding is no longer enough.

You have recognized the knot.
You have traced the threads.
You have seen how it formed.

But clarity alone does not free you.

Severing is not always visible to others.

It is the withdrawal of agreement.
The removal of access.
The reclaiming of authority.

This is the moment when what was tolerated is no longer permitted.
When what was intertwined is separated.
When what once felt necessary is released.

Severing is not punishment.
It is restoration of order.

And once it happens, nothing returns to the way it was.

THE UNBRAIDING PRAYER

Unbraiding inherited entanglements feels disloyal. Because the entanglement was framed as love, family, goodness, faithfulness, respect. So, leaving it can feel like betrayal, arrogance, abandonment, pride, and sin. Even when it's none of those things.

Unbraiding an inherited entanglement does not require condemning parents or rejecting family. It does not require shaming the past or rewriting history. It requires conscious differentiation.

Unbraiding is not accomplished by force. It is accomplished by precision. By awareness. By Spirit-led clarity. By Heaven-backed authority. By the quiet, holy, surgical work of the Holy Spirit.

`This section contains the prayers, declarations, and prophetic activations that release the knots, loosen the cords, untie the threads, and restore the believer to clarity. This is not dramatic deliverance. It is not chaotic warfare. There are no shouting matches with *spirits.*

This is deliverance with dignity. This is healing with order. This is breakthrough with precision.

THE POSTURE OF UNBRAIDING. Before praying, the Believer must position themselves. Become and remain:

Calm - Knots untie faster in peace.

Open - The Holy Spirit is gentle; allow Him access.

Receptive - Freedom is not earned — it is received.

Willing - Some entanglements persist because the person is afraid of the freedom that clarity brings.

Expectant - Knots respond to expectation — not emotion. This posture prepares the soul for spiritual untying.

Following is the unbraiding, unknotting prayer that you've been waiting for. Pray this slowly, intentionally, line by line:

"Father,
I bring my soul before You —
my mind,
my emotions,
my spirit,
my identity,
my assignment,
my dreams,
and my inner court.

Every place where I have been tangled,
knotted,

confused,
pulled,
disturbed,
or spiritually interfered with —
I place it in Your hands.

Untie every knot.
Loosen every thread.
Separate every entanglement.
Undo every crossing.
Break every counterfeit cord.

Unbraid the places where proximity became access.
Unbraid the places where vulnerability invited intrusion.
Unbraid the places where expectation created obligation.
Unbraid the places where emotional transfer entered my spirit.
Unbraid the places where unauthorized access took root.

Restore my boundaries.
Restore my clarity.
Restore my emotional sovereignty.
Restore my spiritual atmosphere.
Restore my identity.
Restore my assignment.
Restore my dreams.
Restore my inner court.

Every thread that is not of You — come loose.
Every thought that is not mine — lift now.
Every heaviness that is not mine — release now.

Every emotional weight that is not mine — fall away.
Every spiritual residue — clear out.

I reclaim my spirit.
I reclaim my mind.
I reclaim my emotions.
I reclaim my authority.
I reclaim my peace.
I reclaim my pace.
I reclaim my purpose.

Lord, unbraid me gently.
Unbraid me fully.
Unbraid me permanently.

In Jesus' Name.
Amen."

THE SEVEN SURGICAL PRAYERS (DIMENSION-BY-DIMENSION)

These are short, precise, surgical prayers that target each dimension individually.

PRAYER 1 — UNBRAIDING THE MIND

"Lord, silence every voice that is not Yours.
Cut every mental loop.
Break every thought that circles instead of settles.
Return my mind to rest. In the Name of Jesus."

PRAYER 2 — UNBRAIDING THE EMOTIONS

"Lord, separate my emotions from theirs.
Identify what belongs to me.
Release what does not.
Reset my emotional center. In the Name of Jesus.""

PRAYER 3 — UNBRAIDING THE ATMOSPHERE

"Lord, cleanse my environment.
Remove every emotional residue,
every spiritual fingerprint,
every lingering weight.
Re-establish Your peace. In the Name of Jesus."

PRAYER 4 — UNBRAIDING THE IDENTITY

"Lord, correct every identity shift.
Restore who I am without this knot.
Re-seat me in my rightful place inside myself. In the Name of Jesus."

PRAYER 5 — UNBRAIDING THE ASSIGNMENT

"Lord, separate my calling from every unauthorized connection.
Realign my purpose.
Return me to my lane. In the Name of Jesus."

PRAYER 6 — UNBRAIDING THE DREAM REALM

"Lord, close every dream gate opened through entanglement.
Remove every intruder.
Sanctify my nights. In the Name of Jesus."

PRAYER 7 — UNBRAIDING THE INNER COURT

"Lord, remove every voice, presence, energy, or influence that sat in a seat You did not assign.
Reclaim Your throne in my inner court. In the Name of Jesus."

AFTER THE UNBRAIDING — THE STILLNESS

Once the prayers have been spoken, a holy stillness enters. This stillness is not emptiness — it is **reclaimed space**. Where the knot once sat, Peace sits. Clarity sits. Identity sits. God sits. This stillness is the signature that the Unbraiding Angel has done its work.

DECLARATIONS AFTER UNBRAIDING

Speak these boldly:

- "My soul is clean."
- "My emotions are mine again."
- "My clarity has returned."
- "My spirit is free."
- "My mind is quiet."
- "My identity is whole."
- "My atmosphere is pure."
- "My lane is restored."
- "Every knot is gone."
- "I am unbraided."

In the Name of Jesus."

CLOSING ACTIVATION: HAND TO HEART

Place your hand over your heart and say:

"I return to myself."
"My soul returns home."
"My spirit stands tall again."
"My peace is restored."
"My clarity is sovereign."
"My assignment is secure."

In the Name of Jesus."

DECLARATION

"I am unbraided — mentally, emotionally, spiritually,
atmospherically, and prophetically.
Every knot that once held me has released me.
I stand in clarity.
I stand in Peace.
I stand in authority.
And I stand in Christ.

In the Name of Jesus."

PART IV

AFTER THE SEPARATION

Freedom does not always feel like relief.

When a knot is severed, something real has been removed.
Even if it was unhealthy.
Even if it was binding.
Even if it needed to end.

Separation changes structure.

What once organized your time, your thoughts, your emotions, your roles — is gone.

And in its absence, there is quiet.
There is space.
There is unfamiliar stillness.

This stage can feel confusing.

You may question yourself. You may miss what was harmful. You may wonder if you acted too quickly or too severely.

But confusion after separation is not proof you were wrong.

It is evidence that something structural has shifted.

This section explores what happens when the noise fadesm and how to remain steady while your internal world recalibrates. Separation is the cut.

Stability is the work that follows.

THE CONFUSION AFTER LEAVING

Freedom does not always feel like relief.
Sometimes it feels like disorientation.

There may be confusion after leaving an Entanglement; there often is.

The confusion stage is where people go back, rewrite history, blame themselves, mistrust what just happened. this chapter is about what happens after the knot is cut when the person realizes:

“Wait… I thought this was normal.”

That is a uniquely post-severing experience.

Most people expect freedom to feel like: relief, clarity, joy, gratitude. But for many, it feels like disorientation, self-doubt, confusion, emotional fog. Not because they miss the person, but because they never knew they were bound. They thought they were loving, loyal, kind, patient, mature, and committed.

So, when the cord is cut, they don’t know what category to place the loss in. They can’t grieve it correctly because they don’t know what it was.

This is not, "I miss them." This is more like, "What exactly just happened to me?" They don't know whether to feel betrayed, foolish, relieved, ashamed, grateful, or angry. So, they feel all of it at once — and often conclude that "Maybe I made a mistake." That's where people re-braid.

They're free…but they don't yet have the language to understand what they were freed from. You cannot grieve properly what you did not correctly identify.

Do not romanticize the past. Don't blame yourself. When God is working, stand back and let Him. Trust God when He intervenes for your deliverance and benefit.

This confusion is evidence of how deep the entanglement was. It is not evidence that the separation was wrong.

They are free, but they don't know what they were freed from. It's like dating or being married to an invisible person -- they were never there. It may make the survivor wonder, "Did I imagine this whole thing?" If you stayed with a seriously flawed person it is because either you or they convinced you that they were not flawed. Perhaps they tried to convince you that you were flawed and they were perfect. Now you come out of that connection and you may feel bewildered. Stop comparing others to this "perfect" person; they are not perfect. Stop comparing others to this imagined FAKE perfection -- and another reason they remain stuck.

The after-effect of entanglement with a person who was never fully present as a person. Not evil. Not imaginary. But structurally absent.

And once the cord is cut, the mind tries to make sense of a relationship that, in hindsight, feels like:

"Was anyone actually there?"

After separation, people don't just miss the person. They realize something far more unsettling: conversations feel one-sided in memory. Decisions were always skewed. emotional labor flowed one way. Presence was inconsistent, selective, or performative. The thought creeps in, *Did I build a relationship with a projection?* That's disorienting because the time, the effort, the feelings were real. But the reciprocal personhood was not.

This creates confusion, not just grief. You can grieve a real person. You cannot easily grieve a role you were playing with someone who never met you there.

So, the mind tries to resolve it by saying, "Maybe I exaggerated the problems." "Maybe I expected too much." "Maybe it wasn't that bad." The alternative is harder to accept, and that is: *I was bonded to someone who was not fully participating in the bond.*

The fake perfection trap is a real thing. Because the person was never fully present, the brain fills in the gaps with idealized memory. They remember potential, moments, glimpses, hopes, what could have been. And they compare every new person to this constructed composite that never actually existed.

This keeps them stuck.

Not in love with the past person, but in loyalty to an illusion. You cannot move forward because you are comparing real people to a person who never fully existed. That's why they remain stalled.

This realization can only happens after separation. While inside the entanglement, they could not see this. Afterward, it becomes painfully clear — but without language, they think they're losing their mind.

They were not foolish. They were trying to relate to someone who never brought their full self to the relationship. That's not stupidity; that's asymmetry. And asymmetry is very hard to detect while you're inside it.

The confusion stage is exactly why people go back into what looks like domestic drama. Outsiders completely misread it because it looks like weakness, low self-esteem, addiction to drama, "she just likes him." It could look like one or both of them are stupid, but this is a spiritual matter.

Internally, the person is actually experiencing disorientation. Silence replaces where there used to be noise. They could be feeling a loss of role, a loss of intensity, loss of purpose, and even loss of identity.

We humans may think or say something very damaging, guess they want to go back until they hurt each other. We shouldn't say that or think it. We need to intercede for the recently unentangled or those who are entanglement resistant.

Even if the relationship was unhealthy, it was structuring. It organized (if not consumed) their time. It organized or heated up their emotions. It organized or fired up their nervous system.

When it's gone, the nervous system panics. What do I do now?

Going back feels stabilizing. It doesn't always feel like romance, but it does feel familiar. *What am I supposed to do without you? We've been together all this time.* Familiar is regulating. Even if familiar was chaotic. The body often prefers known chaos over unknown calm.

That's the confusion stage.

Outsiders, even if they were pulled in to 'help' don't see this. They think, "You said he was terrible." He is, but somehow terrible and regulating can coexist.

That's hard or nearly impossible to explain.

People don't usually return because the relationship was good. They return because the chaos was familiar and the quiet feels foreign. Leaving removes the person. It does not immediately remove the nervous system imprint.

PART V
REORIENTATION OF AUTHORITY

Separation restores space. But space must be governed. When a knot is severed, authority does not automatically return to its proper place. It must be reclaimed, clarified, and exercised.

You are no longer reacting to entanglement. You are learning how to stand without it.

Reorientation is quiet.

It is the steady recognition that:

- not everyone belongs in your inner court
- not every need requires your response
- not every connection deserves access
- not every emotion must be carried

Authority is not control over others. It is governance of yourself.

This section is not about cutting again. It is about keeping what has already been restored. You are not returning to who you were before the knot.

You are becoming someone who recognizes one sooner and does not step into it again.

Freedom is not simply release. It is order maintained.

BUT HOW DID THIS HAPPEN TO *ME*?

How in the heck? How did this happen to me when I am not foolish, not weak, not reckless, or naïve?

You did not get entangled because you were bad at life. You got entangled because you were good at things that knots exploit.

Just because people are looking for these traits in others doesn't mean that they have these traits themselves. The fellow who is interested in you because you are a good person isn't necessarily a good person; he could be looking for a mark. Just because you would look for someone with your same values doesn't mean that everyone or anyone else is. Sorry. There are opportunists in the world. Kindness can become a hook. Loyalty becomes a loop. empathy becomes a cord. Responsibility becomes a tether. Being "a good person" becomes the very thing that attracts them and threatens to entrap you.

What bad person is going to go out to look for another bad person? No, they look for good people, including coming to church to find a nice manageable spouse. Good people get tied in knots because they are good people. It is how you are wired that may attract a narcissist, for example.

Knots – knot makers are looking for virtues to exploit. A person may not even know that they're stuck. They don't know how it happened without them noticing.

Tina or anyone could be thinking, "It's not that I'm bad at adulting...maybe I was distracted. Maybe it is that I was watching and it got me anyway?"

Is there a pride issue? NO, I had my life all planned out and this was not supposed to be part of it.

I'm not the kind of person that this happens to. (Kind of a why bad things happen to good people vibe) so now the person has to fight to un-downgrade themselves for feeling like a failure??

"How did this happen?" and "What does this say about me?" That's the wound people carry out of entanglement. Not just confusion, not just grief. But a quiet, corrosive conclusion such as, I should have known better. I'm not as discerning as I thought. I'm not as strong as I thought. Or, I'm not who I thought I was.

So now, after the cord is cut, after the entanglement is unbraided, they aren't just trying to move forward. First they have to try to undo the shame, undo the self-degradation, and the downgrade of themselves.

After entanglement, the average person doesn't say, "That relationship was unhealthy." Instead, they say, "What is wrong with me that I stayed?" This is when the shame creeps in. That shame is what keeps them stuck long after the person is gone. Pride like, *"I'm not the kind of person this happens to."* So, when it does, the identity crisis is worse than the relationship.

Now they have to reconcile their self-image with their lived experience, and that's painful. This did not happen because you are bad at life, it happened because knots exploit the very traits you value in yourself. You are not just recovering from a bad relationship. You are also recovering from the way it made you see yourself. Correcting this is a powerful and necessary step to healing from the knot dissolution.

The lie you tell yourself after the knot is part of the damage that the knot actually did. You must correct those lies with truths such as:

Tell yourself, say it out loud, "I was not foolish. I was human. And now I am wiser without being smaller."

Sometimes it is shame that they carry within the entanglement or even out of it when they do break free. This is a second injury to the knot itself. What happens when someone is already vulnerable, already disoriented, already seeking help. And then they encounter someone who extracts disclosure without offering safety.

WHY DIDN'T SOMEBODY TELL ME THIS?

There may be anger when the knot victim or survivor thinks, "I DID ALL THE STUFF I WAS TOLD, everything I was taught from a kid until now. So, HOW DID THIS HAPPEN?

Now it feels as if the victim was also lied to and 'set up' for this. the lie after the knot is not just *"What's wrong with me?"* It's also: *"I did everything right. So how did this still happen?"*

That's not self-pity. That's a collision between what you were taught and what actually works in real life. Then you realize the deeper lie: "You were given incomplete instructions for living."

You were taught to be kind, be patient, be loyal, be supportive, be understanding, be forgiving, hold things together, don't quit, don't give up on people.

All of that is good, until you meet a knot.

So the person feels like: *I did what I was told to do. I followed the rules. I lived correctly. And somehow that is what got me here.*

That produces anger. Not at the other person. At the framework they trusted.

This is why the person feels "set up" not by God, of course. They don't feel doomed or set up by fate or by half-truths. The average person was taught how to love.

But, you were not taught how to stop loving when it becomes harmful. That's the missing training. And people feel betrayed by that gap.

Still the lasting feeling may be, "I'm not just sad. I'm mad, because I did everything I was taught to do."

Yes. And that is exactly why this happened. Not as blame — but as explanation. *You were not foolish. You were faithful to instructions but that did not include how to recognize a knot.*

You were trained for connection, not for discernment of unhealthy connection. That's not weakness; that's incomplete preparation. That realization is what lets the anger settle without turning into bitterness.

For 20 years, 20 teachers tell you this, that or the other and then here comes one charlatan and in 2 months you're entangled.... what! You can be well-taught, well-intentioned, well-formed for years… and still be unprepared for one person who does not play by the rules you were trained to live by. That's not stupidity. That's a mismatch of operating systems.

The truth is, you were trained for healthy people. You were not trained for manipulators, takers, or role-*confusers*. All your training assumed mutuality, honesty, reciprocity, and basic goodwill.

A charlatan does not operate on those assumptions. So, all the tools you were given become liabilities: kindness becomes access. Patience becomes time. Empathy becomes entry. Loyalty becomes permission, and forgiveness becomes reset. There you are trying to prove to him what a *nice* person you are. He knows you're a nice person; that's why he's there. He knows your characteristics and your traits are better than the hot girl down the street that you are secretly competing with because you want to win the guy instead of that *femme fatale*. You don't have to bring that to his attention; trust me, he's already seen her.

So this entanglement happens fast, not because you're weak, but because **they** are practiced. You were trained for twenty years to relate to normal people. It only takes two months with someone abnormal to make all that training work against you. You were equipped for healthy relationships, not for people who exploit them.

That's the shock people need explained. Because they keep asking, "How did twenty years of wisdom lose to two months of nonsense?"

Your training didn't let you down. You didn't lose because of it. It was never designed for that *kind* of opponent. That realization is what lets the anger turn into clarity instead of shame. Many Christians are trained to assume honesty, goodwill, and shared values — and are not equally trained to recognize manipulation, deception, or unhealthy dynamics when they appear. That's not "goody-two-shoes." That's trust culture. Trust culture works beautifully among trustworthy people.

I worked with an older man who investigated meter and electricity thefts from the electrical company. He often would say, but in his colorful language, "Oh heck, locks are for honest people."

The problem is when someone enters the picture who performs sincerity, borrows spiritual language, mimics virtue, and does not operate in good faith. So, the problem isn't that believers are naïve. It's that they are trained to extend Grace, not to discern misuse of Grace. We were trained to tell the truth, to be kind, to forgive, to assume the best. We were not trained to recognize when someone is using those very expectations as tools against us.

Once the knot is exposed, the person isn't just thinking, "I was entangled." They're thinking, "Why didn't I see this?" And the answer is because you were trained for healthy people, not deceptive ones.

How many of those 20 people who trained me to be this way--, which should be normal, but didn't serve me well when this wolf came along, are going to help me? Who will help me get out of this? Who will help me repair the damage? Who will help me redeem time or progress lost because of this entanglement?

All the people who trained me for life — where are they now that I'm in ***this****?*

The uncomfortable truth is: most of them can't help you here. Not because they don't care. But because what you're dealing with is outside the framework they taught you. They taught you how to be good, how to love well, how to forgive, how to endure, how to be faithful.

They did not teach you how to disengage, how to recognize manipulation, how to stop over-giving, how to rebuild after being entangled

So, when you look around for help, you often hear: "Just pray about it." "Just forgive." "Just be patient." "Just communicate better." Which is exactly the advice that tightened the knot in the first place.

The people who taught you how to live may not be the people who can teach you how to get out of this. That's not betrayal; it's a recognition that this situation requires a different kind of wisdom.

You are not alone because no one can help you. You feel alone because few people understand what you are facing.

Stand fast therefore in the liberty wherewith Christ hath made us free, and be not entangled again with the yoke of bondage. (Galatians 5:1)

WE NEED JESUS

Not only that, the *kind* of opponent that entangler is, may be the other reason why no one warned you about him. They had never seen such themselves. They had never been taught about such a character at all, so they had nothing to share. They may have secretly just hoped you'd never run up on such, believing or wishing that they are few and far between. You may not even realize until much later what kind of entangler this person even was and what they were working with.

What are you working with? Is another question entirely in today's vernacular. I'm not talking about physical or natural attributes.

People work with spiritual tools that are invisible to the natural eye. If you don't know what idol *god* a person serves and who is empowering them in the spiritual realm, then you don't know what they are working with. So you may meet them, step to them openly and honestly thinking this may be the start of a great friendship or even a romantic relationship. You may even meet them in church and believe they are completely vetted.

Discern every spirit for yourself.

You aren't not working with any hidden agenda therefore you believe they are not as well.

Really?

After you come out of a knot or entanglement the ONLY person who can help you, even if you've had twenty well-intentioned teachers and mentors over the years, is Jesus. He is the only one who can restore your emotions, your soul. He is the only one who can clear away the residue of that relationship. He is the only one who can make it like it was, or even better. Jesus is the only one who can restore the years, redeem the time and accelerate you, if necessary to catch up on lost time and lost progress. No human can.

The fact that it takes Jesus should give you some important clues. One this was a spiritual thing. Entanglements are spiritual. And two, spiritual things do not just happen on their own without any spiritual energy or power or force. If it takes God to break it, then it was pretty powerful. If it takes God to heal it, then it was not only very destructive, there was a dark anointing on the fact that it happened in the first place, or you ignored the discernment and spiritual capabilities you had to keep it from happening in the first place.

Said plainly, due to trust, even in the wrong place, person or system, you laid down your authority and let someone else govern you. We all need Jesus. Every day.

RETURNING TO YOURSELF

Entanglement always creates a sense of internal displacement. You feel off, out of place, unsettled, disoriented, unfocused, emotionally inconsistent, spiritually muted, or mentally scattered. The entanglement didn't just tie you to a person; it pulled you out of yourself and out of alignment with Christ.

The ultimate goal of unbraiding is, of course, to return to yourself. Freedom isn't just the absence of bondage, freedom is the return of identity, clarity, and sovereignty.

1. THE SYMPTOM OF "SELF-DISPLACEMENT"

Entanglement displaces the internal self. You may have felt "I'm not thinking like me." "I don't feel grounded." "This doesn't sound like me." "Why am I so distracted?" "Why am I emotionally inconsistent?" "I don't feel centered."

This displacement is a sign that someone else's emotions entered your emotional space. someone else's spirit sat in your inner court. someone else's influence tangled with your clarity. Someone else's expectations shifted your identity. Someone else's voice diluted your own. Someone else's atmosphere overrode your atmosphere.

Entanglement doesn't just happen TO you — it happens THROUGH you. And the unbraiding brings you **back to your internal seat.**

2. RETURNING TO YOUR MIND

After unbraiding, the first thing that returns is mental quiet. You suddenly notice fewer intrusive thoughts. no more mental circling. decision-making is easier. thoughts feel "yours" again. internal narrative is clean. mental clarity rises. internal silence is peaceful.

You don't realize how loud the knot was until your mind becomes quiet again. This is the sound of your internal sovereignty restoring itself.

3. RETURNING TO YOUR EMOTIONS

When entangled, you didn't know where your emotions ended and theirs began. But after unbraiding your emotions feel "right-sized" again. you feel neutral about the person. Your feelings stop fluctuating. Your emotional center stabilizes. You stop feeling pulled. Guilt disappears. Emotional autonomy returns. Entanglement inflates emotions. Unbraiding resets them.

You realize that what you thought was "connection"… was actually emotional interference. And when the interference is gone, you return to your authentic emotional self.

4. RETURNING TO YOUR ATMOSPHERE

Atmospheric clarity is one of the strongest signs of freedom. When the knot breaks, you experience lighter space, peaceful environment, no more heaviness. no more invisible pressure. You will also notice easier prayer. easier worship, deeper rest, and renewed spiritual sensitivity. You may even be amazed to realize that you had stop hearing from God while you were in this entanglement; almost like you were in a daze. But thankfully, now you are restored and your relationship with the Lord is restored and realigned.

Your atmosphere shifts because your atmosphere was never the problem; the knot was. Atmospheric peace is the signature of spiritual restoration.

5. RETURNING TO YOUR IDENTITY

This is where the **real** homecoming happens. When entangled, your identity was subtly tied to how they saw you, what they expected, the role they placed you in, the emotional contract they created, the energy they projected onto you.

Entanglement creates identity drift. Unbraiding creates identity return. Signs of identity returning are that your confidence rises, your voice returns. your preferences re-emerge. your opinions sharpen. Your boundaries solidify. Your sense of self becomes strong. You stop apologizing for existing. You stop adjusting your presence. Your inner authority activates.

When your identity returns, you finally recognize yourself again.

6. RETURNING TO YOUR ASSIGNMENT

Entanglement always delays purpose. Knots interfere with calling by: absorbing emotional energy, scattering focus, distorting discernment, pulling attention, diverting momentum, confusing direction, clouding intuition. But after unbraiding, your assignment becomes sharp. Your goals realign. Your pace quickens. Your creativity increases. Your vision returns. Your passion reignites. Your spiritual drive awakens.

Your assignment was not lost, it was **interrupted**. And now it's restored.

7. RETURNING TO YOUR DREAMS (LITERALLY)

When the dream realm untangles, dreams become peaceful, no more intrusions, no more spiritual noise, no more nighttime emotions, prophetic dreams return, clarity dreams return, warning dreams return. revelation returns. Your dream realm becomes **yours** again; not shared, not invaded, not interrupted. This is one of the clearest signs the knot has lost its authority.

8. RETURNING TO YOUR INNER COURT

This is the deepest return. Your inner court is where you decide, you feel, you see, you hear, you discern. You anchor. You reign internally

After unbraiding you feel seated inside yourself. you feel "home" in your soul. you feel whole. you feel protected. You feel balanced. You feel centered. You feel sovereign. The place someone else sat is now your place again.

You are back on your own throne. This is spiritual sovereignty restored.

9. THE MOMENT OF RECOGNITION — "I FEEL LIKE MYSELF AGAIN."

This moment is holy.

You will feel calm, grounded, clear, internally quiet. at peace, steady, unbothered, emotionally neutral, and spiritually regulated. You may not even realize until one day you wake up and say, **"Oh. I'm back."**

The knot didn’t just leave; **you returned.**

10. YOU EMERGE STRONGER THAN BEFORE THE ENTANGLEMENT

Because now you have language, discernment, boundaries, emotional intelligence, spiritual skill. the Unbraiding Angel/ the 7-dimension awareness. clarity about your inner court. knowledge of the threads. authority over your own spirit. You did not just survive the entanglement; you OUTGREW it.

You outgrew the version of yourself that could be tangled.

You returned to yourself…as a wiser version.

DECLARATION

“I return to myself.
My identity returns.
My peace returns.
My clarity returns.
My sovereignty returns.
My voice returns.
My assignment returns.
My spirit returns home.
Every part of me that was displaced is restored.

In the Name of Jesus. Amen”

PROTECTING YOUR INNER COURT

The hardest part of healing is not getting free; it is staying free. Once the knot breaks, the spirit must be guarded, the mind must be ordered, the emotions must be regulated, and the inner court must be protected.

Your inner court is the holiest part of you. It is the seat of identity, discernment, intuition, decision-making, self-worth, emotional balance, spiritual authority, and prophetic sensitivity.

This is the place where God meets you. This is the place where clarity is born. This is the place where Truth feels like Truth.

Anyone who is allowed to sit in this seat illegally put you at risk rerouting your entire life. This chapter teaches you how to guard that seat — permanently.

1. WHAT IS THE INNER COURT?

It is your spiritual command center, emotional sanctuary, prophetic intelligence hub, internal throne room, soul headquarters, identity chamber. Think of it like the Holy of Holies inside your spirit.

Only God has permanent access. Only YOU and the Holy Spirit should occupy this space. But entanglements place another person's emotions, another person's spirit, another person's expectations, another person's energy, in that inner sanctuary. To stay free, you must **reclaim**, **reset**, and **guard** that inner court.

2. WHO BELONGS IN YOUR INNER COURT? (ALMOST NO ONE.)

One of the biggest lies of modern spirituality is that:

- "openness is holiness"
- "vulnerability is godliness"
- "shared emotion is healing"

Not true.

Jesus Himself had the crowd (outer court), the 12 Disciples (inner court), and the 3 Disciples who got Holy access. Your life requires the same architecture.

The Outer Court - People you serve, help, work with, talk to.

The Inner Court - A VERY small number of people with earned trust.

The Holy of Holies - Only God. Only you, no one else.

Most people get entangled because they let someone skip levels. Someone jumped from acquaintance to emotional access, from coworker to confidant, from church member to spiritual partner, from friend to inner voice. Your inner court must be invitation-only, and invitations must be rare.

Anna's ex used to ask her all the time, "What are you thinking." She didn't think anything of it the first time it seemed harmless, maybe even intimate. He never asked her that when they were dating or engaged, only after marriage. The second time he asked, she thought this was a little odd but answered him anyway. By the third time and thereafter on the same day, it began to feel invasive. That was persistent demand for access to unspoken interior space.

Anna didn't have anything to hide, she just felt that every thought is not public property. She didn't have the language for it then, but she felt that her inner court was being treated like a hallway.

There are places inside you that are reflective, forming, processing, listening. They are not secrets. They are sacred. Access to that space is not automatic. It is earned. When someone demands entry without invitation, something in you tightens. That tightening is information.

Eventually, Anna would just answer him with a Bible verse. *Why*? Because Scripture is safe language. It creates boundary without confrontation. Anna was protecting her inner court before she even knew what it was.

Someone asking you what restaurant do you want to go to versus simply asking, in moments of silence, as many as three or four times a day, *What are you thinking,* is no longer casual curiosity. That becomes *monitoring*. It is not necessarily malicious — but it is regulating.

A request for emotional transparency on demand is not normal. It appears to be a need to manage a person's internal state. It is a subtle signal: "Your private thoughts make me uneasy." Or, is what I'm doing evident to you (yet). It is a way of trying to control the relationship.

Anna felt that. It felt invasive. Not that she was hiding anything but interior space is not communal space.

Not every forming thought belongs in the public square. There is a difference between sharing and being monitored. The inner court is where thoughts are still forming. It is not a space for interrogation.

Dear Reader: Intrusion, emotional, spiritual or any other kind doesn't have to sound rude or look dramatic. It can look polite. It can seem intimate or spiritual, but it can still be too much.

The Progression of Entanglement

Thread
Proximity
→ Familiarity without discernment
→ Emotional Seduction

Thread
Vulnerability
→ Emotional access too soon
→ Emotional Seduction

Thread
Expectation
→ Invisible obligation
→ Identity Distortion

Thread
Emotional Transfer
→ Carrying what isn't yours
→ Spiritual Confusion

Thread
Access
→ Influence over inner world
→ Identity Distortion

THE FIVE GUARDRAILS OF THE INNER COURT

These five guardrails prevent future knots.

Guardrail 1 — Emotional Discernment. Ask yourself: "Does this person bring Peace or pressure?" If someone repeatedly drains, confuses, obfuscates, distracts they are not bringing Peace. Does this person cause you to shrink or withdraw? Do you feel a tightening in your spirit or a shift in your mood?

Ask, "Does this person affect your focus?"

"Does this person make your mind noisy?"

If the answer is yes to those questions, then they should not be allowed into emotional proximity. Your spirit speaks through comfort and discomfort. Listen.

Guardrail 2 — Access Control. Access should be earned, not assumed. Ask:

- How much have they proven?
- How consistent are they?

- How do they hold boundaries?
- Do they respect your time?
- Do they respect your NO?
- How do they handle distance?
- Do they honor your peace?

If access creates chaos, **access must be revoked.**

Guardrail 3 — Pace Regulation. One of the fastest ways people entangle themselves is by moving too quickly emotionally or spiritually.

Regulate the pace of emotional sharing, spiritual sharing, personal conversation, vulnerability access, and connection development.

Speed, being rushed is a trap. Slow is safe. If someone pushes emotional pace or spiritual intimacy too quickly — it's a red flag.

Guardrail 4 — Boundary Enforcement. Set your boundaries firmly, not soft boundaries. Not polite boundaries. Not hinted boundaries. **Clear, unapologetic, unapologized-for boundaries.**

Examples:

- "I do not share that part of my life."
- "I don't talk after these hours."

- “I’m unavailable for emotional processing today.”
- "I'm not the right person for this conversation."
- “I am not your spiritual covering.”
- “I cannot be that role in your life.”

Boundaries prevent knots before they form.

Guardrail 5 — Identity Anchoring

The more rooted you are in WHO YOU ARE, the harder it is for anyone to entangle you.

Identity anchoring includes:

- knowing what you want
- knowing what you don’t want
- knowing your emotional capacity
- knowing your spiritual assignment
- knowing your pace
- knowing your boundaries
- knowing your non-negotiables
- knowing what your spirit rejects

People who know who they are do not get knotted easily. Identity confusion is entanglement soil.

Identity strength is entanglement armor.

4. THE INNER COURT TEST: 10 QUESTIONS

If you want to know whether someone belongs in your inner court, ask:

1. Do I feel peaceful after interacting with them?
2. Do I feel like myself around them?
3. Do I feel spiritually clear around them?
4. Do I feel pressured to respond or maintain connection?
5. Do I trust them with my silence?
6. Do they respect boundaries without offense?
7. Do they amplify my identity instead of altering it?
8. Do they honor my assignment instead of competing with it?
9. Do they give more than they take?
10. Is God present in the relationship or merely tolerated?

If even **three** answers are "no," they cannot enter the inner court. If **five** answers are no, they cannot remain in your outer court. If **eight or more** answers are no, you are already entangled.

5. EMOTIONAL HYGIENE: KEEPING YOUR SPIRIT CLEAN

Just like physical hygiene, emotional hygiene requires routine care. Daily practices to protect your inner court:

Morning Reset

"Today my spirit is mine."

Midday Check

"Who entered my mind and why?"

Evening Closure

"I release everyone from my emotions today."

Prayer of Sovereignty

"Lord, keep me centered in You, and clear on who I am."

Quiet Hours

Times when the world has no access.

Sacred Solitude

Not loneliness — replenishment.

Emotional Fasting

Take a break from people who drain or destabilize.

Your spirit needs quiet like your body needs water.

6. PROTECTING YOUR INNER COURT FROM FUTURE ENTANGLEMENTS

Don’t over-explain yourself.

Over-explaining is an early sign of a knot forming.

Don’t overshare emotionally.

Vulnerability requires boundaries.

Don’t spiritualize chemistry.

Chemistry is not covenant.

Don’t let ministry roles replace identity discernment.

Just because someone serves you doesn’t mean they know you.

Don’t reward emotional intensity with access.

Intensity is not intimacy.

Don’t confuse familiarity with trust.

Familiarity forms faster than trust.

Don’t ignore inner alarms.

Your spirit knows long before your mind understands.

7. WHEN GOD GUARDS YOUR INNER COURT FOR YOU

Sometimes God removes someone. Suddenly, they leave, they withdraw. communication breaks. the connection dries up. They disconnect. circumstances shift

You didn't do it; GOD did.

Why?

Because God protects assignments. God protects momentum. God protects clarity. God protects identity. Sometimes God ejects people who would've become knots. Don't take it personally. Take it prophetically.

8. THE FINAL SHIFT — YOU BECOME YOUR OWN PROTECTOR

After unbraiding, something powerful happens: You stop needing to be rescued. You stop needing warnings. You stop needing signs. You stop needing external reminders.

You *feel* the threads at the earliest stage. You sense the tug before it becomes a pull. You notice the atmospheric shift immediately. You recognize emotional crossing as soon as it happens.

Your spirit becomes a high-security zone with:

- clarity at the gates

- discernment at the walls
- boundaries at the doors
- identity on the throne

No one enters illegally again.

DECLARATION

"My inner court is holy.
My inner court is protected.
My inner court is guarded by peace, clarity, and the Holy Spirit.
No one enters without assignment.
No one sits in a seat God did not give.
I protect my spirit.
I guard my emotions.
I honor my identity.
I defend my atmosphere.
And I remain untangled.

In the Name of Jesus, **Amen**"

THE REBRAIDING

Unbraiding is not the end. Unbraiding is the **reset. Say it, realize it, know it:**

"I am not just free — I am RE-BRAIDED. In the Name of Jesus, Amen."

Once the threads loosen, once the cords break, once the knot dissolves, once the spirit returns to clarity and peace… God begins His work. The **rebraiding.**

This chapter is the revelation of what God does AFTER freedom. It is about how He restores, renews, reweaves, redirects, rebuilds, reassigns, and realigns. God never leaves His daughters and sons untied — not tangled, not loose, not floating.

He reweaves. He re-reestablishes. He recommissions. Divine design has always been first the unbraiding, then the healing. Next is rebraiding and then thriving, in Christ.

Unbraiding → Healing → Rebraiding → Thriving

1. WHAT IS REBRAIDING?

Rebraiding is God's process of:

- reweaving your identity
- re-centering your spirit
- re-anchoring your purpose
- re-aligning your relationships
- re-stabilizing your emotions
- re-establishing boundaries
- re-strengthening your clarity

Rebraiding is **divine reconstruction**. It is the holy, gentle, intentional work of the Father as He braids your life together, this time with **Him**, not with an entanglement.

3. GOD BRAIDS WITH PURPOSE — NOT WITH PEOPLE.

A counterfeit cord ties you to a person. A Divine cord ties you to assignment, clarity, identity, peace, purpose, promise. **God does not braid you INTO someone; He braids you INTO purpose.**

The Threefold Cord is:

1. **You**
2. **God**
3. **Your assignment**

Not you, God, and a random individual. Not you, God, and an emotional connection. Not you, God, and a false bond. God's braid is never chaotic, confusing, heavy, and never fog-filled.

His braid is firm, steady, sure and pure. It is aligned, and peaceful. You feel SAFE in a Divine braid never pulled, pressured, or disturbed.

4. THE FIRST STRAND OF REBRAIDING: IDENTITY.

This strand returns first. After unbraiding, God says **"This is who you are."** Suddenly you feel your confidence rise. Your voice strengthens. Your worth increases. Your authority activates. Your internal "spine" returns. your emotional posture straightens.

You remember who you were and who you are, who you are becoming. Identity becomes the anchor strand of the new braid.

5. THE SECOND STRAND OF REBRAIDING: PEACE

Peace is not just an emotion; it is a spiritual environment. Peace is the original atmosphere of the soul. Before Adam sinned, he walked in Peace. Before the knot, you walked in Peace.

After unbraiding, God reweaves Peace into your core. Peace becomes your climate, your protective layer, your boundary, your internal voice, your emotional filter, your discernment ground, your spiritual compass

Peace returns you to equilibrium.

With Peace restored, you can hear accurately, think clearly, choose wisely, sense properly. Peace is the second strand of the Divine braid.

5. THE THIRD STRAND OF REBRAIDING: PURPOSE

Purpose returns LAST — not because God is slow, but because God must rebuild identity and peace FIRST.

Why?

Because you cannot carry assignment while knotted. You cannot discern direction while fogged. You cannot steward calling while emotionally hijacked. You cannot launch destiny while spiritually entangled.

Once identity and Peace are braided back into place, the final strand appears: Purpose.

Suddenly creativity flows, ideas spark, momentum returns, clarity aligns, open doors become visible, distractions fall silent, assignments feel natural, and direction becomes obvious.

Purpose is the final sign you have been rebraided.

AFTER REBRAIDING: YOU BECOME UNTANGLEABLE

Once God rebraids you, you become:

- Unhookable,
- Unshakeable,
- Unmanipulable,
- Unemotionally Hijackable,
- Undistractable,
- Unentangleable,
- Unconfusable

Your spirit becomes firm, settled, mature, discerning, centered. Before you were porous, now you are fortified.

Where before you were available to everyone, now you are reserved for your assignment. Where before you absorbed, now you observe.

Where before you merged, now you maintain sovereignty. Where before people could tie into you, now they bounce off your walls.

You become spiritually **knot-proof**.

7. SIGNS YOU ARE FULLY REBRAIDED

This is how you know:

You feel emotionally neutral

Not cold — just sovereign.

You feel spiritually stable

No waves, no noise, no pull.

You feel mentally quiet

Thoughts shut up. Peace takes over.

You feel identity-solid

Your inner voice is stronger than outer voices.

You feel steady

Grounded. Balanced. Rooted.

You feel unavailable to dysfunction

Low-quality connections cannot access you.

You feel aligned with purpose

Your "yes" is clean.
Your "no" is firm.
Your direction is clear.

You feel like YOU again

Not the tangled version.
The original version.

8. GOD NEVER LEAVES YOU WITH LOOSE THREADs

This is the comfort.

God doesn't just unbraid what the enemy tangled. He **rebraids what the enemy tried to destroy**.

He gathers your dignity, your clarity, your peace, your authority, your insight. your intuition, your identity, your wisdom. your emotional intelligence, your discernment, your assignment …and braids them into a **new version of you**.

He improvs you into a version that can't be knotted again in the same way. A version that is spiritually and emotionally upgraded. You are prophetically upgraded. You are identity-upgraded.

You are now a version that carries **internal sovereignty**.

9. THE FINAL CALLING OF THE REBRAIDED

Once God rebraids you, you carry a mantle of discernment, clarity, emotional intelligence, spiritual sobriety, boundary-setting, prophetic accuracy, internal order, and identity strength.

You become a walking **untangling instrument**. People feel lighter around you. People feel clearer around you. People feel safe around you. People feel God's Peace when they talk to you. People receive revelation simply by hearing you speak.

The rebraided become **liberators.** Because they carry clarity and clarity is contagious.

10. FINAL DECLARATION — THE REBRAIDING SEAL

Place your hand over your heart and say:

"I receive the divine rebraiding of God.
I receive my identity back.
I receive my peace back.
I receive my purpose back.
My soul is woven with God.
My spirit is aligned with truth.
My assignment is reconnected.
I am whole.
I am restored.
I am rebraided.
And I will never be tangled again.

In the Name of Jesus, **Amen."**

I seal this book, all words, decrees, declarations and prayers herein across every realm, age, era, dimension, and timeline, past present and future and to infinity. I seal them with the Blood of Jesus and the Holy Spirit of Promise.

Let every retaliation against this word, these prayers, these decrees and declarations spoken, prayed, or said by the speaker, or heard by the listener, or anyone praying these words backfire without Mercy, to infinity against the evil perpetrator, in the Name of Jesus. **Amen.**

Dear Reader

Thank you for acquiring and reading this book, I pray it has blessed you as you allow the Spirit of God to break you out of every entanglement.

Shalom,

Dr. Marlene Miles

Prayerbooks by this author

There are some books that are only prayers. You just open up the book and pray.

Prayers Against Barrenness: *For Success in Business and Life*

Fruit of the Womb: *Prayers Against Barrenness*

Beauty Curses, *Warfare Prayers Against*
https://a.co/d/5Xlc2OM

Courts of Marriage: Prayers for Marriage in the Courts of Heaven *(prayerbook)* https://a.co/d/cNAdgAq

Courtroom Warfare @ Midnight *(prayerbook)*
https://a.co/d/5fc7Qdp

Demonic Cobwebs *(prayerbook)* https://a.co/d/fp9Oa2H

Every Evil Bird https://a.co/d/hF1kh1O

Gates of Thanksgiving

Spirits of Death, Hell & the Grave, Pass Over Me and My House

Throne of Grace: Courtroom Prayer

Warfare Prayer Against Poverty https://a.co/d/bZ61lYu

FAKE FRIENDS: *Prayers Against Betrayers*

HOLIDAY WARFARE Prayer Manual (humorous) Surviving Family Gatherings All Year Long (without catching a case)

SOUL TIE Prayer Manual (The) Part of a 3-part series including a workbook.

MAD at DADDY Prayer Manual – part of a 3-part series including a workbook.

Healing the Sibling & Relative Wound Prayer Manual

Healing the Father-Son Wound Prayer Manual

Prayers Against Barrenness: *For Success in Business and Life*

Breaking Curses of the Mother Prayer Manual

Other books by this author

Abundance of Jesus (The) https://a.co/d/5gHJVed

AK: The Adventures of the Agape Kid

Already Married in the Spirit: *Why You May Not Be Married in the Natural*

AMONG SOME THIEVES https://a.co/d/dkYT4ZV

Ancestral Powers

Anti-Marriage, *The Spirit of*

Backstabbers https://a.co/d/gi8iBxf

Barrenness, *Prayers Against* https://a.co/d/feUltIs

Battlefield of Marriage, *The*

Beware of the Dog: Prayers Against Dogs in the Dream.

Bless Your Food: *Let the Dining Table be Undefiled* *https://a.co/d/6oPMRDv*

Blindsided: *Has the Old Man Bewitched You?* https://a.co/d/5O2fLLR

Break Free from Collective Captivity

Broken Spirits & Dry Bones

By Means of a Whorish Father

Caged Life: Get Out Alive! https://a.co/d/bwPbksX

Casting Down Imaginations

Christ of God (*The*) 3-book series

Christ of God, (*The*) Box Set, includes all three books

Churchzilla, The Wanna-Be, Supposed-to-be Bride of Christ https://a.co/d/eAf5j3x

Collateral Damage: *When What Happened Spiritually Was Your Fault*

Demonic Cobwebs (prayerbook)

Demonic Time Bombs

Demons Hate Questions

Devil Loves Trauma, *The*

Devil Weapons: Unforgiveness, Bitterness,...

The Devourers: Thieves of Darkness 2

Do Not Swear by the Moon

Don't Refuse Me, Lord (4 book series)

https://a.co/d/idP34LG

Dream Defilement

The Emptiers: *Thieves of Darkness, 1*
https://a.co/d/5I4n5mc

Evil Touch

Failed Assignment

Fantasy Spirit Spouse https://a.co/d/hW7oYbX

FAT Demons (The): *Breaking Demonic Curses*
https://a.co/d/4kP8wV1

The Fold (5-book series)

- The Fold (Book 1)
- Name Your Seed (Book 2)
- The Poor Attitudes of Money (3)
- Do Not Orphan Your Seed (4)
- For the Sake of the Gospel (5)
- My Sowing Journal

Gang Ups: Touch Not God's Anointed

Gathered: No Longer Scattered
https://a.co/d/1i5DPIX

Getting Rid of Evil Spiritual Food

https://a.co/d/i2L3WYQ

got HEALING? Verses for Life

got LOVE? Verses for Life https://a.co/d/8seXHPd

got HOPE? Verses for Life

got money? https://a.co/d/g2av41N

Has My Soul Been Sold? https://a.co/d/dyB8hhA

Here Come the Horns: *Skilled to Destroy* https://a.co/d/cZiNnkP

Hidden Sins: Hidden Iniquity

https://a.co/d/4Mth0wa

How to Dental Assist

How to Dental Assist2: Be Productive, Not Wasteful

How to STOP Being a Blind Witch or Warlock

I Take It Back

In Multiplying I Will Multiply Thee

Irresistible: Jesus' Triumphal Entry
https://a.co/d/d09IfEC

KNOW YOUR BATTLE: Stop Swinging Blindly — and Win Against Opponents, Adversaries & Enemies (Workbook) https://a.co/d/eOwFKlV

Legacy

Let Me Have A Dollar's Worth https://a.co/d/h8F8XgE

Level the Playing Field

Living for the NOW of God https://a.co/d/6bK5duE

Lose My Location https://a.co/d/crD6mV9

Love Breaks Your Heart

Mad At Daddy: Healing Father-Wounds that Affect Motherhood (book, workbook & prayer manual)

Made Perfect In Love

Mammon https://a.co/d/29yhMG7

Man Safari, *The*

Marriage Ed.: *Rules of Engagement & Marriage*

Made Perfect in Love

Money Hunters: Beware of Those

Money on the Altar https://a.co/d/4EqJ2Nr

Mulberry Tree, *The* https://a.co/d/9nR9rRb

Motherboard (The)- *Soul Prosperity Series*

Name Your Seed

Occupy: *Until I Return* https://a.co/d/bZ7ztUy

Opponent, Adversary, or Enemy?: Fight The Right Battle with the Right Weapons

https://a.co/d/byQqEE2 & companion workbook: Know Your Battle

Plantation Souls

Players Gonna Play

Portals: Shut the Front Door: Prayers to Close Evil Portals.

Power Money: Nine Times the Tithe

https://a.co/d/gRt41gy

The Power to Get Wealth https://a.co/d/e4ub4Ov

Powers Above

The Robe, Part 1, The Lessons of Joseph

The Robe, Part II, The Lessons of Joseph

Seasons of Grief

Seasons of Siege: God Is Coming

Seasons of Waiting

Seasons of War

Second Marriage, Third--, *Any Marriage*

https://a.co/d/6m6GN4N

Seducing Spirits: Idolatry & Whoredoms

https://a.co/d/4Jq4WEs

Shut the Front Door: *Prayers to Close Portals*
https://a.co/d/cH4TWJj

Sift You Like Wheat

Six Men Short: What Has Happened to all the Men?

SLAVE

Sleep Afflictions & Really Bad Dreams
https://a.co/d/f8sDmgv

Soul Prosperity soul prosperity series 3

https://a.co/d/5p8YvCN

Soul Ties: How Soul Ties Form, and How To Break Them (book, workbook & prayer manual)

Souls In Captivity

The Spirit of Anti-Marriage

The Spirit of Poverty https://a.co/d/abV2o2e

Spiritual Thieves https://a.co/d/eqPPz33

StarStruck- Triangular Power series.

SUNBLOCK- Triangular Power series.

The Swallowers: *Thieves of Darkness,* 3

Take It Back

This Is NOT That: How to Keep Demons from Coming at You

Time Is of the Essence

Too Many Wives: *Why You Have Lady Problems*

Tormenting Spirits https://a.co/d/dAogEJf

Toxic Souls

Triangular Power *(series),* Powers Above, SUNBLOCK, Do Not Swear by the Moon, STARSTRUCK

Unbreak My Heart: *Don't Let Me Die*

Uncontested Doom

Unguarded Hours, *The*

Unseen Life, *The* (forthcoming)

Upgrade: How to Get Out of Survival Mode Toxic Souls (Book 2 of series) , Legacy (Book 3 of series)

The Wasters: *Thieves of Darkness,* Bk 2 https://a.co/d/bUvl9Jo

What Have You to Declare? What Do You Have With You from Where You've Been?

When I Was A Child, *I Prayed As a Child*

When the Devourer is Rebuked

https://a.co/d/1HVv8oq

WTH? Get Me Out of This Hell https://a.co/d/a7WBGJh

The Wilderness Romance ***(series)*** This series is about conducting a Godly relationship and marriage with someone who is a Wilderness person. It is about how to recognize it and navigate through it. These books are about how not to get caught up in such.

- ***The Social Wilderness***
- ***The Sexual Wilderness***
- ***The Spiritual Wilderness***

Other Series

The Fold (a series on Godly finances) https://a.co/d/4hz3unj

Soul Prosperity Series https://a.co/d/bz2M42q

Spirit Spouse books

https://a.co/d/9VehDSo

https://a.co/d/97sKOwm

Battlefield of Marriage, The

https://a.co/d/eUDzizO

Players Gonna Play

https://a.co/d/2hzGw3N

Sent Spirit Spouse (can someone send you a spirit spouse? This book is not yet released.)

Matters of the Heart, Made Perfect in Love https://a.co/d/7OMQW3O , Love Breaks Your Heart https://a.co/d/4KvuQLZ, Unbreak My Heart https://a.co/d/84ceZ6M Broken Spirits & Dry Bones https://a.co/d/e6iedNP

Thieves of Darkness series

The Emptiers https://a.co/d/heio0dO

The Wasters https://a.co/d/5TG1iNQ

The Swallowers https://a.co/d/1jWhM6G

The Devourers: Why We Can't Have Nice Things https://a.co/d/87Tejbf

Spiritual Thieves

Red Flags: The Track Is Not Safe (book & workbook)

Triangular Powers https://a.co/d/aUCjAWC

Upgrade (series) ***How to Get Out of Survival Mode*** https://a.co/d/aTERhXO

We Get Along, Right? Compatibility for Couples – (book & workbook)

Dr. Marlene Miles is a teacher, author, and spiritual thinker known for her grounded, discerning approach to prayer and spiritual formation. Her work emphasizes clarity, restraint, and maturity in faith—helping believers move beyond emotionalism and performance into a steady, practiced walk with God.

With a deep respect for Scripture and a practical understanding of daily life, Dr. Miles writes for those who want their prayer life to be formed, not dramatized. Her teaching encourages spiritual maintenance, discernment, and responsibility—so faith remains strong not only in crisis, but in everyday living.

www.ingramcontent.com/pod-product-compliance
Lightning Source LLC
LaVergne TN
LVHW010951110826
845149LV00015B/3293

* 9 7 8 1 9 7 1 9 3 3 2 8 3 *